I Love Lucy

TV Milestones

I LOVE LUCY

Lori Landay

TV MILESTONES SERIES

Wayne State University Press   Detroit

18 17 16 15 14   6 5 4 3 2

Library of Congress Cataloging-in-Publication Data

Landay, Lori.
I love Lucy / Lori Landay.
p. cm. — (Tv milestones)
Includes bibliographical references and index.
ISBN 978-0-8143-3261-0 (pbk. : alk. paper)
1. I love Lucy (Television program) 2. Situation comedies (Television programs)—
United States. I. Title.
PN1992.77.I253L36 2010
791.45'72—dc22
2009042580

This book is dedicated to my mother, Sheila Landay,
who loves to laugh at Lucy, and to my sons Jason and Sammy,
because if Lucy had had twins, now *that* would have been funny.

CONTENTS

ACKNOWLEDGMENTS

I have been working on the Lucy phenomenon for a while, and ix many people offered valuable feedback on earlier versions of this material. I presented papers at MIT's Media in Transition 3 in 2004 and the Media Ecology Association conference in 2006, where David Marc pointed my research in a better direction. My first Society for Cinema and Media Studies (then SCS) paper was on *Lucy,* and SCMS members, especially Janice Welsch, have been a source of information and community. The team at University of Pennsylvania Press, where I published *Madcaps,* helped me turn a dissertation into a book. Mary Dalton and Laura Linder, the editors of *The Sitcom Reader: America Viewed and Skewed,* helped sharpen my argument. Annie Martin, acquisitions editor for Wayne State University Press, worked patiently to bring this book to fruition. The two anonymous reviewers for the press offered criticism that strengthened the project. The series editors, Barry Grant and Jeannette Sloniowski, helped shape the book. Christopher Anderson, my professor at Indiana University at the inception of this project in his 1990 seminar, Media Institutions and the Production of Culture, continues to provide quick, accurate, and always witty answers about 1950s television. Susan Gubar, also my professor at Indiana, continues to be an influential mentor and friend; hardly a day goes by that I don't think about how she taught, or something she said.

I am fortunate to work at Berklee College of Music, which has been very supportive of me personally and professionally. Many people encouraged this book there, especially Janet Chwalibog, Camille Colatosti, Charles Combs, Peter Gardner, Kathy Zerlin, William Banfield, and Bertram Lehmann. I owe Zoe Rath, a librarian at Berklee's Stan Getz Library, special thanks for years of quick and cheerful assistance. I would also like to thank our provost, Larry Simpson, for asking his trademark thought-provoking questions.

Many people made it possible for me to complete this project, especially "Team Twins": Coralie Cooper, Jill and Jim Cownie, Nancy Gordon, Suzanne Hanser and the Hanser-Teperow family, Marty Harrison, Jonathan Landay, Myrna and Roger Landay, Lauren Pitalis, and especially my parents, Sheila and Charles Landay. My husband, Richard, a wonderful partner in all things, provided editing help, good humor, and overall support.

I am particularly lucky to have Shujen Wang in my life as both a colleague and friend. She read the entire manuscript, made substantial suggestions about structure and organization, and in general made this book and my life better. When I was writing about female friendship, I thought about her, and about Lauren, Coralie, Jenny, Chris, Phyllis, Tammy, Patty, and Michelle.

My students, particularly in Approaches to Visual Culture, have been enthusiastic about Lucy TV, reminding me how different television culture is now than it was then. This book is written for them, to answer their excellent and challenging questions about how culture works and why some things change and some things don't.

Some 'Splainin' about Lucy TV

"Lu-cy! You've got some 'splainin' to do!" These words, **1** half-sung by an irate Ricky Ricardo who can't believe that his wife Lucy has done it *again,* echo throughout the television milestone series *I Love Lucy.* How did *I Love Lucy* do it again and again, redefining what it meant for a character, a television show, and an entire industry to be popular in mainstream American culture? This is the main question at the heart of the cultural phenomenon of *I Love Lucy.*

I Love Lucy aired 180 episodes as a weekly sitcom from 1951 to 1957 (and the characters appeared in thirteen hour-long specials that aired from 1958 to 1960); in those six seasons, the top-rated show "splained" the conventions of the sitcom, of television culture, and of the wider postwar culture, all within the context of what we can call "Lucy TV": how Lucille Ball came to embody the promise and popularity of the new medium because of a confluence of Lucille Ball's comic talents, the plasticity of the new medium, the rapid adoption of television in the home, the domestic focus of the content of television, and the savvy way in which the creative team behind and in front of the cameras brought together the traditions of the stage, radio, and cinema to shape the conventions of television.

The concept of "Lucy TV" also speaks to how television audiences and popular discourses of television personalize television; it is a medium of personality and intimacy. Of course, no single person—a star—is individually responsible for the success of a television series, or even for the creation of a star persona, but there is the tendency to collapse the considerable amount of creative, technical, and business talent and work into a few recognizable individuals, and part of the I Love Lucy mythos is indeed that telescoping: Desi Arnaz gets the credit for all the business and technical innovations, and Lucille Ball gets the credit for the comedic genius, when in fact they both were the public faces of highly successful collaborations of groups of people. Further, the publicity surrounding I Love Lucy lingered over the details of Lucille Ball and Desi Arnaz's real-life marriage that were incorporated into the series' depiction of Lucy and Ricky Ricardo, minimizing any differences between the stars and their characters.

The term "Lucy TV" also encompasses the unity of television culture in its infancy, when there were only three or four channels, depending on the local market, so the television audience was not fragmented in the way it is today. As television was making inroads into American homes and lives, I Love Lucy was skyrocketing to previously unattainable levels of popularity and market penetration; the April 7, 1952, episode "The Marriage License" was the first television program to be seen in ten million homes, at a time when there were a total of fifteen million television sets in operation in America. At its crucial initial phase, television was indeed "Lucy TV."

Moreover, the magazines and newspapers that covered television were literally covered with Lucy; in the spring of 1952, Lucille Ball and her hit television show were featured on the covers of major national magazines, including Time, Newsweek, Life, Look, and Cosmopolitan. When Ball's real-life pregnancy was incorporated into the series in the 1952–53 season, I Love Lucy redefined what it meant for a television program to be popular, with the episode in which the baby was born, "Lucy Goes to the Hospital" (January 19, 1953), the most-watched television show ever at the time. The broader phenomenon of Lucy TV became so intertwined with television that the first issue of the weekly magazine *TV Guide* (April 3, 1953) had a picture of Lucille Ball and Desi Arnaz's baby on it. Throughout the series' run, it never fell out of the top three rated shows, and its popularity persists today.

What is it about *I Love Lucy* that made it such a success, a milestone in the emerging medium of television? There are many factors that we'll explore throughout this book, but some stand out: an efficient production system, a compelling narrative formula of likable characters and clever plots within a familiar situation, hilarious writing, magnificent comic performance, remarkable chemistry, and technical genius that brought it all together and preserved it on film. The setup of Ricky Ricardo, a bandleader from Cuba, and his screwball American wife, Lucy, living in an apartment in New York alongside their landlords and best friends, Ethel and Fred Mertz, has more permutations than one might initially imagine. Even after the initial situation shifted with the arrival of a baby halfway through the second season, the Ricardo and Mertz visits first to Hollywood in the fourth season and then to Europe in the fifth, and the foursome's move from the city to Connecticut in the sixth and final season, the relationships between the characters that are enacted with comic brilliance remain at the heart of the show.

In order to explore the series from its inception to its final form as hour-long specials, this book is organized both chronologically and thematically, with a spotlight placed on specific issues and cultural contexts where they seem most appropriate. Overall, the book takes an interdisciplinary, cultural studies approach to understanding the wider phenomenon of Lucy TV, which means thinking about the processes through which culture works: how a television show is created, produced, circulated, advertised, viewed, understood, enjoyed, remembered, and reinterpreted. Some of the theoretical and multidisciplinary approaches to media studies used in the book include feminist theory, cultural anthropology, cultural analysis, media institution history, social history, textual analysis, and genre criticism.

The book is structured into chapters that follow the series from its origins to its end, with particular emphasis on the issues and contexts that different phases of the series suggest. The first chapter is "Television in the Home and the Home on Television: Fifties TV and Lucy TV," because television is a particularly *domestic* medium experienced primarily in the home, and makes the case for placing *I Love Lucy* in a broad cultural context. The second chapter, "Origins of *I Love Lucy:* Authorship and Production Contexts," zooms in on the series' inception at a formative stage of the television industry; it documents some of the business and technical innovations that Ball and Arnaz's production company Desilu developed that had a big impact on audiovisual style. The discussion of how *I Love Lucy* shaped early television and the genre of the situation comedy continues in the third chapter, "Narrative and Comedic Conventions and Innovations of the Situation Comedy: The Basics of Lucy TV," which focuses on the narrative and comedic breakthroughs achieved in this milestone series; it analyzes the continuities and differences with Ball's radio show *My Favorite Husband* to set up a discussion of the genre of the sitcom. The fourth chapter, "Trickster Lucy: Popularity, Comedy, Gender, and Culture," takes the focus of comedy from the previous chapter and brings Lucy TV into a broad cultural discussion of storytelling and character types, specifically the trickster. The fifth chapter, "A Spotlight on 1953: Lucy TV in Its Cultural Context," turns our attention to the year of the peak of *I Love Lucy*'s popularity and some major cultural currents in which Lucy TV was made and received—the baby boom, discourses of ethnicity and race, and the anticommunist blacklist—by examining specific episodes that shed light on—or attempt to hide—the thorny issues of the time. The final chapter, "The End of *I Love Lucy* and Beyond," relates how the series ended with hour-long specials made while Ball and Arnaz were on the brink of divorce, and touches briefly on the other Lucys that Ball portrayed in the sitcoms she made after *I Love Lucy;* the chapter and book conclude with a reflection on the persistent popularity of Lucy TV around the world today.

Chapter 1

Television in the Home and the Home on Television

Fifties TV and Lucy TV

Imagine watching *I Love Lucy* in 1951. Television was very new, not yet in every household, let alone in almost every room, so maybe you are watching at your house or apartment, or maybe at a friend's or family member's house. The characters on your screen inhabit a living room with a television set; you are watching them watching television, and television is rapidly becoming an essential part of everyday life. This is the backdrop to the cultural phenomenon of "Lucy TV," and to better understand it this chapter explores the place of television in the post–World War II home and how the home was portrayed on television, specifically on the most popular television series of the 1950s, *I Love Lucy.*

The Center of the Home

When television emerged as a mass medium in the early 1950s, American culture found a new physical and social center of the home, what media critic Marshall McLuhan called an "electronic hearth"[1] (qtd. in Marc and Thompson 55). But in contrast to the traditional center of heat, food, and family activity, the new hearth connected the home and the outside world,

Television is at the center of the home in "The Courtroom."

bringing images, sounds, stories, and people into the everyday lives of Americans. Home-decorating magazines of the late 1940s and early 1950s depicted the television set replacing the baby grand piano as the centerpiece of the ideal living room, with the piano shown as an upright off against a wall or relegated to a less-prominent room. The television was not only an object to gather around, as indicated by the title of the 1946 book *Here Is Television: Your Window to the World*; the book suggests that television erases the boundaries between the home and the world. To be sure, seeing events rather than only hearing about or reading about them created an immediacy that made the outside world more accessible. However, those images were mediated and framed by the discourses of television culture: the television program created within specific production and cultural contexts and also watched within particular domestic, technological, and cultural frameworks. Television was not simply a "window to the world"; it was (and is) a locus of powerful cultural work that, as media theorist Stuart Hall postulated, encodes meanings, interpretations, and values that people decode within their homes and in the contexts of their beliefs and social experiences.

The Television Set

In order to understand what television meant in the 1950s, first we need to think about the television apparatus itself: the item, the picture, where it was, and how people watched it. In these days of big color screens, it is hard to imagine how small and blurry the television image was in the early 1950s. Television screens were typically ten to twelve inches wide and showed black and white, and the reception of the broadcast image was not the clear picture we have come to expect from digital cable and satellite. Viewers had to tune in the signal over the airwaves and adjust the antenna to help sharpen the signal. Moreover, the sets themselves were expensive (an average of $279 when the average price of a new house was under $10,000) and big and heavy (like a chest of drawers); some even had cooling systems and needed to be watered (Marc and Thompson 54).

Despite the small picture and uneven quality, television quickly became common in American homes; in 1950 only 9 percent of homes had television sets, but by 1955 more than 65 percent of homes had them. Several factors led to the rapid adoption of the new medium: set prices dropped from around $440 in 1948 to about $230 by 1954; the growth of suburbs, where people often lived far from their extended families; a new emphasis on an ideal of the nuclear family in the postwar period; and the idea of television watching as a family activity taking place in the suburban home. With most families having only one television set and programming offered on only three or four channels, television viewing during the "antenna age" fostered social cohesion, or at least common cultural references and experiences. In contrast to today's cable, satellite, internet, and DVD sources of television programs, 1950s television culture was unified. In 1952, *Variety* reported that *I Love Lucy* was seen by a record twenty-nine million viewers a week (based on an average of 2.9 viewers per home in ten million homes), more than twice the average audience that sees a Hollywood movie in its domestic first run (Sanders and Gilbert 59).

A large part of television programming was "live" television, which was unprecedented in its ability to bring the audience a sense of immediacy, reality, and participation. Radio certainly could broadcast live, but listeners had to use their imaginations, their "radio eye," to quote a 1927 print ad for RCA radio tubes. By adding the visual element, television was perceived as more "real" than any other medium, in part because of the way it was integrated into everyday life (as opposed to the specialness of the filmgoing experience). Sounding a lot like Walter Benjamin exulting in the possibilities of film in his 1936 essay, "The Work of Art in the Age of Mechanical Reproduction," many commentators in the 1950s noted the medium's unique aspects, echoing Benjamin's observation that

> the film, on the one hand, extends our comprehension of the necessities which rule our lives; on the other hand, it manages to assure us of an immense and unexpected field of action. Our taverns and our metropolitan streets, our offices and furnished rooms, our railroad stations and our factories appeared to have us locked up hopelessly. Then came the film and burst this prison-world asunder by the dynamite of the tenth of a second, so that now, in the midst of its far-flung ruins and debris, we calmly and adventurously go traveling. (236)

For example, Jack Gould, the television writer for the *New York Times* in the 1950s, commented that live television "removes from an audience's consciousness the factors of time and distance. . . . Live television . . . bridges the gap instantly and unites the individual at home with the event afar. The viewer has a chance to be at two places at once. Physically, he may be at his own hearthside but intellectually, and above all emotionally, he is at the cameraman's side" (qtd. in Boddy 80).

I Love Lucy was not live television, but it retained some of the aspects of live television. Stylistically, by inventing the system of editing footage from three cameras filming simultaneously in front of a live audience, the series' creative team tried to combine the immediacy of live television (via radio) with the narrative conventions of cinema, including continuity editing. Part of the cultural phenomenon of "Lucy TV" are the techniques of making television that mark a signpost on the way to "hyperreality," the slippage between the real and the imaginary posited by postmodern theorists like Jean Baudrillard and Umberto Eco, where reality and representation implode. Where does the reality of performers in front of an audience end and the artifice of cutting between different camera positions begin? Or, in a series about a married couple starring the really married Lucille Ball and Desi Arnaz, where do the actors end and the fictional Lucy and Ricky Ricardo begin? The answers that the show posits are distinctly different from what research into the production and publicity contexts tells us. This is indicated perhaps most viscerally by hearing the sound of the audience laughing—and sometimes being able to hear Desi Arnaz's distinctive laugh offscreen as Lucille Ball performs Lucy's antics in scenes that do not include Ricky's presence—one of many frames that sought to make connections between "reel life" and real life.

Television on Lucy TV

Advertising, magazines, and television itself made the placement, style, and attitude toward the television set a topic of discourse.[2] It must have been profoundly strange to purchase a television set and suddenly have strange people and distant places "in" your living room. For example, in a wonderful sequence from one of the best *I Love Lucy* episodes, "Lucy Makes a TV Commercial" (May 5, 1952, which culminates in her Vitameatavegamin drunken act), Lucy physically inserts herself into the television chassis to demonstrate to Ricky that she would be great on TV. The levels of television narratives and frames are multiple: Lucille Ball, star and spokesperson for sponsor Philip Morris cigarettes, acting the part of Lucy Ricardo, acting the part of a Philip Morris spokesperson inside a television in the Ricardo living room, which is on the television in the spectator's living room. Ball calls attention to the permeability of these boundaries between home and television when Lucy leans out of the television frame to pick up the cigarettes she has dropped. When Ricky enters and tries to "turn the channel," Lucy pushes his hand away from the knob. In this scene, Ricky and Lucy enact the myth, the fantasy, of the immediacy of television and make comedy out of the intersections of home and television.

The Home on Lucy TV

So far we have considered the television in the home; now let's turn to the image of the home that was represented on those televisions. When we think of 1950s TV, especially sitcoms,[3] we tend to think of an idealized domesticity. This is the world of what media historian David Marc wittily termed the "WASP-com" (*Comic Visions* 54) that was satirized in the film *Pleasantville* (1998), of the polite, white, middle-class families of shows like *Father Knows Best* and *Leave It to Beaver* whose problems are always solved by the end of the half hour. The fantasies of mid-1950s sitcoms were a powerful factor in creating the ideology of postwar life, but family life wasn't really like that any more than family life is accurately portrayed on television today. A 1994

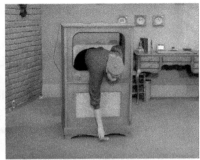

Lucy crosses the boundaries between television and the home in "Lucy Makes a TV Commercial."

study of demographics from 1950 to 1989 concluded that there was little convergence between the fictional families portrayed on television and real families (Douglas 13). Nevertheless, the portrayal suggests an ideal, and because television exploded at a time of a turn toward domesticity and family life, those ideals became very influential.

The depiction of the home and domestic life in *I Love Lucy*, like other pre-1955 television representations, presents a messier kind of domesticity, one in which patriarchal control over the home was contested by Lucy's unwillingness to submit to being a good little wife content in the home. Moreover, Ricky's ethnic identity as a Cuban American is one of the last vestiges of the ethnic comedy so popular on radio and early television. Unlike the suburban homeowners of *Father Knows Best* and *Leave It to Beaver*, the Ricardos were apartment renters in the city who often struggled and squabbled about money. Rather than an atmosphere of plenty, *I Love Lucy*'s comedy was often rooted in scarcity—of money (albeit not for food or rent, but for middle-class commodities and status) and of attention (mostly Lucy's desire for it). Because of its locus in both the domestic and performance (or "show business") spheres, *I Love Lucy* also contrasted celebrity with "ordinary life," an opposition born out of the show's grappling with ideas about authenticity and immediacy.

To be sure, television viewers were used to seeing the home portrayed in the movies and on radio, but level of detail of domesticity and intimacy in home life and marriage depicted in *I Love Lucy* went far beyond the representation in film. Looking at the first half-dozen episodes of the first season, we see many scenes played out in the Ricardo bedroom; in the pilot, we see Ricky shaving as if the camera were the mirror. Perhaps this focus on the bedroom was acceptable because Ball and Arnaz were married in real life. Nevertheless, there is time in the weekly half-hour sitcom to show the minutiae of everyday life in a way that is beyond the narrative conventions of film. The sponsor's frame further wraps the episode in the habits of everyday life (including, in the case of *I Love Lucy*, smoking the sponsor's cigarettes), as does its place within the "flow" (to use Raymond Williams's term) of the television programming that precedes and follows it.

Television and the Home Have a Lot in Common

For example, let's look at how the relationship between domesticity and television is represented in "Mr. and Mrs. TV Show," a fourth-season episode that aired on April 11, 1955, in which

Lucy and Ricky star in a husband-and-wife show set in their home. The plot begins with Lucy trying to support Ricky's career by convincing an advertising agency executive that Ricky should be on television. Lucy assumes that they will both be on the show, because it was her idea and "It's my chance to go coast to coast." Ricky retorts, "I love this country. It's been very good to me. I wouldn't think of doing a thing like that to my fellow citizens." But when Ricky meets with the advertising executive, a comic figure who takes credit for everyone else's ideas, the only format in which he is interested is a husband-and-wife show, *Breakfast with Ricky and Lucy*. Ricky convinces Lucy it was he who insisted that the show include her and be in the husband-and-wife format. In a stylistic departure from the visual and narrative conventions of the series, Ricky begins the show within the show by directly addressing the camera, "Hello there, I didn't see you come in," as if the viewer were a guest joining him; Lucy enters in a lovely nightgown and robe set, praising the sponsor's products, again looking into the camera.[4] Fred and Ethel enter and sing a jingle about the sponsor, Phipps Department Store. The testimonials continue. But after the rehearsal, when Lucy finds out that it wasn't Ricky's idea to include her, she decides to teach Ricky a lesson during what she thinks is the rehearsal, but the show is being broadcast live. Lucy subverts the version of the show we saw earlier by saying terrible things about the department store's products and services, putting Ricky (who knows the show is live) on the spot, and then dresses up in a burlap bag with a fright wig as the makeover she had at the department store salon. Of course, the sponsor wants nothing more to do with them and Lucy ruins her chance at having a television show.

The plot reinforces the image of television as a domestic medium, but it also exposes the portrayal of home life on television as staged and inauthentic. Lucy and Ricky's "real" way of being at home is imperfect, comfortable, and often filled more with bickering than politeness. In this way, the episode makes comedy out of the clash between the idealized television text and the "reality" of Lucy and Ricky that we have come to know over the years of the series (this episode was in the fourth season). Instead of their usual comfortable-looking pajamas (available for sale as just one of the many Desilu commodities), Ricky and Lucy wear fancy nightclothes, are overly polite, and eat a fancy breakfast in the dining room when we know they usually eat breakfast in the kitchen. Like other episodes that focus on advertising and television, including the famous Vitameatavegamin act in "Lucy Does a TV Commercial," this episode reveals that television is an advertisement for the sponsor. Every time Lucy and Ricky light up a Philip Morris cigarette, they are advertising the sponsor and depicting cigarette smoking as a natural part of the good life. It is cultural hegemony in action.

Thinking about *I Love Lucy* as an advertisement for Philip Morris instead of entertainment shifts the way we interpret the series, and popular culture in general. The entire narrative strategy of early television blurred the boundaries between the sponsor's product, the fictional diegetic world of the show, the actors, and the audience. By doing what "Mr. and Mrs. TV Show" exaggerates and satirizes, *I Love Lucy* and other television series incorporated the sponsor's commodities seamlessly, and in many ways, cigarettes are the ultimate commodity—addictive, fetishized, available in neat little packages, branded, and profitable.[5] By exaggerating the television personalities plugging the sponsor's products, the episode obfuscates how the characters and the actors participate in advertising.

Moreover, "Mr. and Mrs. TV Show" is a good example of how a television text is contradictory. On the one hand, the episode makes fun of sponsorship, advertising, and television, exposing the television text as a thin veneer to con the audience. However, the episode also portrays television as transparent. There is no special set or lighting for the show within the show, or wardrobe, or makeup, or writers. Unlike the show within the show, the narrative and visual style of the series, reinforced by continuity editing and other elements of classical Hollywood style, maintain the diegesis as "real." When the characters smoke they do not need to refer blatantly to "Philip Morris" because the sponsor's introduction to the episodes, the animated openings, and pattern of the stars' role in print and television advertisements have already, subtly, made those connections.

On yet another level, the episode plays self-reflexively with reality. In the fictional world, the adman is only interested in Ricky if his wife is a part of the deal, but in real life, as anyone who read any of the hundreds of newspaper and magazine stories that had circulated by the fourth season of the series certainly knew, it was Ball whom the network and advertising agency wanted, and she refused to star in a show without her husband. So, the lie Ricky tells Lucy is the true story of their portrayers, but reversed. This extratextual knowledge from one of the aspects of the Lucy phenomenon gives the audience member another way of interpreting the episode, creating an even greater intimacy with the stars by being "in" on the joke.

17

Back to the Home?

I Love Lucy represented television in a contradictory manner, and it depicted the home similarly. The series is set primarily in the Ricardo apartment, with many episodes also having scenes set at Ricky's club and the Mertzes' apartment; when Lucy, Ricky, Fred, and Ethel "go" to Hollywood, their hotel suite becomes the major locale, and when they all move to Connecticut in the sixth and final season of the half-hour format, it is their suburban home at the center. Throughout the series, the home is the site of the characters' relationships, especially between Ricky and Lucy, but also between Lucy and Ethel, between the two couples, and less often, between Ricky and Fred. It is Lucy's responsibility as wife to keep the house clean, cook and serve the meals, and maintain a pleasant and comforting atmosphere to which Ricky returns. Despite her trickiness and attempts to escape the confines of the home and the role of housewife, Lucy is presented as capable in maintaining the home. However, when it comes to finances, Lucy routinely overspends the household budget and the allowance she receives from Ricky. Her desires for something more extend to the home as well as her career, and she is interested in upgrading their furniture and other domestic possessions, often measuring her home against external standards. In all these ways, *I Love Lucy* depicted the home according to hegemonic domestic ideology, as a site primarily of labor for women and leisure for men.

One of the first episodes, "Men Are Messy" (December 3, 1951), exemplifies the series' representation of the home. Lucy has just finished cleaning up the Ricardo living room when Ricky comes in and, in about two minutes, strews clothes, banana peels, newspaper, and papers everywhere, moving the plants and knickknacks Lucy had so carefully placed. When pressed, Ricky explains, "A man's home is a his castle, and this is my castle." In order to teach him a lesson (a common impulse in the series), when Lucy knows their home will be photographed for what she thinks is a musician's magazine and only seen by people who know Ricky, Lucy dresses like a hillbilly in overalls and transforms the apartment into "Tobacco Road" with clothes hanging on a line, trash cans, tires, and even live chickens. (*Tobacco Road* was a 1941 John Ford film that relied on stereotypes of hillbillies as crude, lazy, and filthy.) Unfortunately, Lucy doesn't realize that the photographer is from the popular mainstream magazine *Look,* not from the musician's magazine. The article is flattering to Ricky, with pictures of him at the club, but despite the photographer's promise not to use any of the Tobacco Road pictures in the articles, Lucy is on the cover in her hillbilly getup, looking very different from the glamorous, well-groomed image Lucy likes to portray. This is only one of a multitude of performances that Lucy enacts as the opposite of the good, companionate wife who helps her husband's career and provides a sanctuary for him in the home, and her comeuppance is that she is publicly humiliated as the opposite of a good wife and woman.

In addition to the battle of the sexes at the center of the conflict between Lucy and Ricky (and of course Fred and Ethel take their gender-mate's side), this episode highlights two other recurring themes of the series: the desire for fame and the rejection of feminine beauty for comic effect. One of the big differences between Lucy and Ricky is that he is a celebrity, and indeed his celebrity status becomes a central preoccupation of the series, especially in the Hollywood story arc when Ricky is cast in a movie as the "new Valentino." The fascination with celebrity is interesting because throughout their professional

Lucy suffers for violating the domestic ideal in "Men Are Messy."

lives, Ball was the bigger star; as we'll see in the next chapter, although television producers were eager to star her in a television series, they needed to be convinced that husband Desi Arnaz should be costar. It is almost as if the fictional life of the couple was an inversion of their actual relative status, and enabled them to play out a fantasy of more conventional gender roles.

The use of a mockup of a *Look* magazine cover also points to how *I Love Lucy* incorporated commodities other than the sponsor's cigarettes in its diegesis, or narrative world. *Look* magazine, like *Life,* and other mainstream national magazines, often featured Ball, Arnaz, and the show on its cover and in its pages, offering the audience an important source of extratextual information about Ball and Arnaz's marriage, children, home life, past careers, and behind-the-scenes knowledge of the making of the show. The Desilu publicity machine was effective and far-reaching, making sure that there was considerable print media coverage of the show and its stars and controlling the stories that emerged about them. When we think of a series that depends on magazine publicity to enhance its popularity prominently featuring magazine coverage in its fictional world (and several episodes revolved around Lucy inadvertently making Ricky look bad in front of reporters, or on television like in "Mr. and Mrs. TV Show"), we can see the series contributing to the importance of the secondary texts in the *I Love Lucy* phenomenon. This was especially true in the 1953 synchronized births of both Lucy and Ricky's fictional baby and Ball and Arnaz's real-life son (discussed in chapter 5).

In "Men Are Messy," Ball transgresses the lines that demarcate ideals of femininity by deliberately looking ugly, acting in an uncouth manner, and showing off a messy home. This episode is a good example of how the character Lucy functions as a trickster figure. As we will see in chapter 4, Lucy's trickery, like that of all trickster figures, often backfires, making her the dupe. Like many screwball heroines of 1930s film comedies,

Lucy uses disguise, costume, makeup, language, and man-nerisms to perform cross-class, cross-race, and cross-gender impersonations that call attention to the boundaries between those socially constructed categories.

As a trickster, Lucy transforms the home from a site of wom-en's labor into a performance space in which gender, ethnicity, class, region, and other aspects of identity are fluid. But the comic possibilities of the Ricardo home are layered on top of the conventional domestic space, and although the *Look* article does not use the photographs of the messy apartment, Lucy pays for transgressing the domestic ideal with public humilia-tion. Although there are some aspects of domestic ideology that *I Love Lucy* provides an opening to question, the importance of the home and television's place in it were not among them. With its popularity, *I Love Lucy* became a powerful force for the central role television played in postwar American culture, both shaping and reflecting the television in the home and the home on television.

Origins of *I Love Lucy*

Authorship and Production Contexts

The creation of *I Love Lucy* tells us a lot about the television industry in the early years. Part personal mythology and part business negotiations, the story begins with the combination of Lucille Ball's hit radio show *My Favorite Husband* and the real lives of Ball and her husband, Desi Arnaz. Throw in startling innovations in television narrative and style adapted from film and live theater, and you get the groundbreaking, convention-setting, wildly popular *I Love Lucy*. The creation and production of *I Love Lucy* provide a context in which we can better understand the Lucy phenomenon, its significance for television history, and its meaning in American culture.

Origins in Radio

The series debuted in 1951, when broadcast television was still in its infancy. Since her first movie role in 1933, Lucille Ball had achieved some success in movies, but was never really a big star; she was known as "Queen of the Bs"—B-movies, that is. Ball pushed through to the A-list on radio, though, with her successful starring role in *My Favorite Husband*, which ran from 1948 to 1951, and maintained a movie career. But it was in television that Ball really became a star, and found a role and medium that changed media history forever.

Many popular radio programs were being turned into television shows in the late 1940s and early 1950s. From the 1920s, radio was broadcast into people's homes and occupied a central place in domestic life, with programs ranging from news, sports, and quiz shows to adventure serials, dramas, and, as they were called, "domestic comedies" set in the home. *My Favorite Husband* was one of the first radio comedies to move from a vaudevillian model to what came to be known as "situation comedy," with logic behind the comic business. As *My Favorite Husband* and *I Love Lucy* producer and writer Jess Oppenheimer explained, he and writers Madelyn Pugh and Bob Carroll Jr. broke new ground with their radio sitcom, "We just weren't writing what was then considered the 'in' kind of radio comedy show, where you have a series of comedy characters, each of whom comes in, does his own shtick, and then exits. Instead, we did whole stories—*situation* comedy" (*Laughs* 127–28).

Radio situation comedy developed within the medium's production context. Radio audiences in the "golden age" of the 1930s and 1940s were accustomed to the idea of sponsorship, and programs were often made by advertising firms for corporate sponsors who bought air time from a network; *My Favorite Husband* was produced by the advertising agency Young and Rubicam, who hired the creative talent and oversaw the process, owned and paid for by General Foods, and sponsored by Jell-O.

Stars were expected to do commercials during the broadcast. Oppenheimer recalled, "When General Foods bought the program, the sponsor made it clear that it wanted Lucy to be its spokesperson on the show. In addition to starting every program by saying 'Jell-O everybody,' Lucy was expected to do a Jell-O commercial at the end of each episode." In fact, the economics of radio production prompted Ball to develop one of her signature bits when she created her trademark "spider" "eeww" voice doing a Jell-O ad based on doing nursery rhyme characters: "When we did 'Little Miss Muffet,' Lucy, as the Spider, contorted her face into a teeth-baring grimace and came out with a high-pitched, nasal voice that had the audience howling" (Oppenheimer, *Laughs* 126).

National radio networks like CBS were "common carriers" that broadcast the programs made by advertising agencies to affiliated local stations, but the radio model of production was not economically viable because of television production's much more complicated and expensive system. Instead of agencies or local stations producing their own programs, the networks brokered deals, using their own advertising agencies to work with corporate sponsors, but overseeing the production themselves. TV stations couldn't afford not to affiliate. Because 98 percent of television stations were affiliated with the national networks, "American television emerged literally overnight as a genuine *mass* medium" (Schatz 119).

25

Ball and Arnaz?

When CBS first approached Ball about doing her radio show on television, she suggested that Arnaz be her costar and that they broadcast the show live from the West Coast (where she and Arnaz lived). Like Ball, Arnaz had had some success as a film actor without ever really becoming a big star (they first met at the RKO lot and worked together on *Too Many Girls* in 1940 and married soon after), and Arnaz also had a popular radio show as a Latin bandleader, a cultural type in which he was typecast because he was Cuban. CBS was not interested in doing the show outside of New York and, famously, CBS executive Hubbell Robinson did not think that American audiences would accept that the "All-American typical redhead" Lucille was married to, as Desi put it, "a Latin bandleader with a 'Cuban Pete' conga drum 'Babalu' image" (Sanders and Gilbert 28).

"But we *are* married," Ball protested, according to the many accounts of the show's origin that proliferated in mainstream magazines and newspapers in 1951 and 1952. Determined to work together, the couple asked *My Favorite Husband* writers Madelyn Pugh (one of the very few women writers of the time and someone who would write for Ball for the rest of her career) and Bob Carroll Jr. to work up a vaudeville act, which they took on the road in the summer of 1950. The audience's positive response across the country convinced CBS chairman William Paley to agree to make a series pilot costarring Ball and Arnaz and produced in California. Ball's radio producer and writer Jess Oppenheimer joined the team, working with Pugh, Carroll, Ball, and Arnaz to turn the stage show into domestic comedy. The pilot, shot live on video before a studio audience, pleased CBS, and their ad agency Biow Company sold the series to the tobacco company Philip Morris. Then conflict arose: Biow expected the series to be shot in New York at the CBS studio, so they could control it and also because broadcasting the show live from Los Angeles meant only a fraction of the national audience would see it live on the West Coast while the rest of the country, which held 85 percent of the audience, would get a kinescoped picture of inferior quality.

Still, Ball and Arnaz held on to their dream of working together on the West Coast, and the result of this intersection of the personal concerns of the couple, the flexibility of the new television medium, the narrative conventions inherited from radio and theater, and the economic and organizational constraints of television production and advertising reveals a lot about the complex process of innovation. Arnaz, president of the couple's production company Desilu, continued hard negotiations to use film, which he thought would give him creative control. Eventually CBS agreed that the show could be shot on film if it was performed before a live studio audience, but at a pay cut for Ball and Arnaz to fund the extra costs. Arnaz concurred, but only if Desilu retained full ownership of the series after its first network showing; the combination of having the shows on film and owning the rights to them meant that Arnaz had invented the premise for reruns and residuals. Although Arnaz said he didn't realize the ramifications at the time, he certainly made a savvy business deal, one that, in the words of media scholar Thomas Schatz, "affected the emergent TV industry on various fronts" (120).

The Desilu Production System

The system that Desilu proposed borrowed aspects of film, radio, and live theater production and created what Schatz, well known in film studies for exploring "the genius of the system" of the mode of production in the Hollywood film studios, terms a new "economy of production design" (123), with limited sets, only a few characters (like on radio sitcoms), and recurring plots. A whole new production system had to be invented around the use of film for television shows, which had to be rehearsed, filmed, and edited in one week; even the lowest-budgeted movies took at least four to six weeks. Desilu was not alone in this, and contrary to popular myth, the film industry was open to television production and the "telefilm" developed as the dominant form of television narrative; in the same 1951–52 television season in which *I Love Lucy* debuted, there were several telefilm series, including *Dragnet* and *Amos and Andy.* It was common for actors who had some success in radio, like Ball, to set up their own production companies to produce their own series, which fostered the development of independent production. Live programs were still the majority in the early 1950s, but the success of *I Love Lucy* and other shows established the Hollywood telefilm as a viable form (Anderson 68).

Filming the show presented many obstacles, and Arnaz turned to a specific "genius" to give his system the right look and technical requirements. Arnaz hired Academy Award–winning film cinematographer Karl Freund, who was part of the wave of German expatriates who came to Hollywood in the

1930s and had been the cinematographer for many silent films, including landmark of expressionism *The Golem* (1920) and Fritz Lang's masterpiece *Metropolis* (1927), and after he moved to Hollywood, Ball's 1942 MGM movie musical, *Du Barry Was a Lady*. "Papa" Freund, as he was known, had the reputation of being an innovative and creative problem solver. Instead of using the standard single-camera filmmaking techniques, which resulted in nonsequential camera, set, and lighting setups (with the camera moved and lighting reset between each shot), Freund developed a three-camera setup that allowed the episode to be shot as a play, with continuity and shot in real time, and with as few camera setups as possible. He suggested that they shoot on a film studio soundstage rather than on a theater stage, which Desilu modified to hold bleachers for the audience. He also pioneered a system of overhead lighting that was uniform (necessary for the three cameras to work simultaneously) and that also flattered Ball. Freund even chose the paint color for the sets, so they would photograph well, trying out many shades of gray until he found the right ones.

Freund also came up with a creative solution to edit the footage; he connected three film-editing machines, as Ball later recounted: "One night [Freund] brought us to his house in the valley and showed us the system he'd invented for us, one that could film simultaneously on three cameras and then, when the show was over and the film was developed, you could sit in the cutting room and his machine played back all three shots simultaneously, so you could cut from one shot to another" (qtd. in Schatz 123). Other sources, including Oppenheimer, credit film operations manager George Fox with inventing the "three-headed monster," as the special Moviola machine that could run the sound track and the three cameras' footage at one time came to be called.

Freund evolved a shooting system that used three BNC Mitchell cameras with T-stop calibrated lenses on dollies. The middle camera covered the long shot using twenty-eight- to fifty-millimeter lenses. The two close-up cameras, seventy-five to ninety degrees apart from the center camera, were equipped with three- to four-inch lenses, depending on the requirements for coverage. Freund developed special long lenses to keep the cameras far enough away from the actors so that the studio audience, in stadium-seating bleachers, could see what was going on. Freund explained, "Retakes, a standard procedure on the Hollywood scene, are not desirable in making TV films with audience participation. . . . Close-ups, another routine step in standard filmmaking, were discarded since such glamour treatment stood out like a sore thumb."

I Love Lucy is often credited as the first television show to use the three-camera system, but that is not quite accurate. The game show *Truth or Consequences* used three cameras to film in front of an audience, and so Desilu hired the person who developed that system, Al Smith, to be their production manager. Previously, in 1950, producer Jerry Fairbanks created the "Multicam" system of using three film cameras on tripod dollies to approximate the quick continuous shooting style of video cameras, but the budgets of the various dramatic series he shot didn't allow him to run all three cameras at the same time. By only having one camera running at a time, Fairbanks did not have the editing issues that *I Love Lucy* film editor Dann Cahn and his assistant Bud Molin faced. Cahn and Molin's solutions resulted in a system of cutting between the footage that established conventions still used today.

Narrative and Audiovisual Style

The new economy of production design developed by Freund, Cahn, and Molin resulted in a specific narrative and audiovisual style, one that could utilize a few permanent sets, uniform lighting, moving multiple cameras rather than many single-camera setups, and continuity so the performance made sense to the audience. "Filmed live in front of a studio audience" meant that the production team put on a real show every week, again borrowing from radio and theater. Arnaz's band played between the scenes, and Desi warmed up the audience, telling jokes and introducing the cast, with Ball always last. Part of the "love" of the show is the audience response, and we are placed within that live audience by the audiovisual style. When we hear Arnaz's distinctive laugh from offscreen in a scene that Ricky is not in, we are included in that live performance. When what we see moves between the different camera positions, we inhabit two different but complementary spatial relationships to the characters. Because the proscenium arch is preserved, we are reminded that we are watching a staged play; by varying our proximity to the actors, we experience a kind of freedom from physical limitations at the same time that we become accustomed to new limitations.

Stylistically, camera placement, movement, framing, and editing also built each scene's and the episode's climax. It combined the proscenium-preserving spectator's point of view from live theater with the principles of film continuity editing. It placed the spectator physically where he or she had been aurally in radio. The camera movement and editing allowed the point of view to move into particular places in the domestic space of the Ricardo apartment, preserving the continuity of space. Comic framing is usually from the medium shot and farther. Slapstick and pratfalls in particular require a full-body shot because close-ups can compromise the emotional distance we need to perceive comedy; if there were a close-up of a person's face slipping on the banana peel, we would focus on the subjective experience of the person, not on the spectacle. We need to see the whole body, or much of it, interacting with its environment and manipulating space and time, for effective comedy.

On the other hand, Ball's brilliant comic muggings required some close camera positions, albeit not close-ups as they are used in film (in part because the three-camera setup didn't allow for close-ups that had the same visual style as the rest of the footage). The directors, Freund, and the film editors developed a rhythm of moving closer to the actors, a language of camera positions that ranged across a smaller spectrum than the long shot to extreme close-up continuum of classical Hollywood cinema, moving between the medium close-up (waist up), medium shot (whole human figure), medium long shot (farthest the camera goes, to show the whole living room, Tropicana club), with some close-ups (neck and up), especially of Ricky singing in the club.

In this sequence of images from the opening scene of "Job Switching," an episode we'll analyze in detail in the next chapter, we can see how the three cameras provide three different shots (the four-shot and then the gender-divided two-shots). The editing underscores the narrative, with the men and women divided visually, with each pair presenting its side of the comic argument that results in the men and women agreeing to change places, with the men taking care of the homes and the women doing a wage-labor job.

Just as I Love Lucy pioneered a distinctive look, it also created the conventions for a distinctive sound. The convention for early television shows was for a scene to cut to black and then for the commercial to come on with a completely different audiovisual style. Desi Arnaz found this change too abrupt and opted for an "integrated" style of commercial, with his I Love Lucy orchestra making the transition from the show to the commercial by continuing the score into the bridge and into the commercial. Always business-minded, Arnaz made it part of the deal with Philip Morris to integrate their commercials, and soon other companies were asking Desilu to do the same for them. This became an income stream for the company for many years, and the practice of using music to integrate the commercials became the standard convention for commercial

Camera shots dramatize the battle of the sexes in "Job Switching."

television, and part of what makes music (and Arnaz's music in particular for *I Love Lucy*) such an integral aspect of the overall style of a specific series.

Desilu Publicity Machine's Creation Story, or the Popular Version of the Origin of Lucy TV

Audiences knew about the show's creation story, or at least the highlights; the relentless Desilu publicity machine made sure of it. After its initial October 1951 debut, *I Love Lucy* quickly skyrocketed in the ratings, soon achieving unprecedented popularity and hitting the number one spot in February 1952. In that month, there were stories on *I Love Lucy* that mentioned the salient details of the production context: that Ball and Arnaz were really married, that they owned their own show, that the show was based on details from their marriage, that the show saved their marriage because they were able to work together. As *I Love Lucy* rocketed to the top of the ratings in its first season, feature stories, including cover stories, appeared in popular magazines and newspapers, including *TV Guide, Time, Newsweek, Life, Look,* the *New York Times, Cosmopolitan,* and many more.

Indeed, it would have been hard to watch the show and not already know that the stars were married in real life. Several critics have suggested that the reason why the characters' beds are pushed together in the first season (until Lucy's pregnancy makes the implied sex life too visible), in contrast to the use of double beds in other television and film depictions, is because of their real-life marriage. Certainly the knowledge about the "real life" of the stars encouraged the illusion of intimacy between the audience and the characters on the show. What is often missing from the publicity materials is the fact that a majority of the scripts for the first two seasons were based on *My Favorite Husband* radio scripts (written by the same team of producer Jess Oppenheimer and writers Madelyn Pugh and Bob Carroll Jr.), with some long exchanges of dialogue word for word, before the baby shows sent the writers into new material. So although anecdotes about how Ball and Arnaz liked the bedroom at different temperatures, which become gags in the Ricardo bedroom, give audiences a context, many of Ball's fans might have recognized some familiar material.

Jack Gould, one of the most perceptive television critics of the 1950s, described *I Love Lucy's* appeal in March 1953: "'I Love Lucy' is as much a phenomenon as an attraction. Fundamentally, it is a piece of hilarious theatre put together with deceptively brilliant know-how, but it also is many other things. In part it is a fusion of the make-believe of the footlights and the real-life existence of a glamorous 'name.' In part it is the product of inspired press agentry which has made a national legend of a couple which two years ago was on the Hollywood side-lines" (16).

The "inspired" publicity machine that Gould mentions was unremitting and effective. Of the hundreds of magazine and newspapers articles and features on which my research is based, rarely do any deviate from the official Desilu publicity machine's story of how television saved their marriage. The basic story is: Ball and Arnaz were so busy with their separate careers that they barely saw each other for the first ten years of their 1940 marriage. They wanted to work together, especially when many successful radio shows were transitioning to television, and there were other popular husband-and-wife teams, like George Burns and Gracie Allen. But producers were reluctant to develop projects for them due to Arnaz's Cuban ethnicity and strong Spanish accent. Ball and Arnaz went on the road across America with a vaudeville act to prove that the audience liked them, but they canceled the second half because Ball was pregnant at age thirty-nine. Although she had a miscarriage, she was soon pregnant again, so they hid her six-month-along pregnancy with a baggy bathrobe and filmed the pilot episode. The sponsor (Philip Morris) and network (CBS) picked up the show and began production only a month after their daughter Lucie was born.

The technical innovations of the production context are discussed in the articles—that Desilu Productions owned the show and it was filmed live before a studio audience—but the articles foreground the love story. For example, a March 1952 *Chicago Sunday Tribune* article explained: "Desi and Lucille are particularly grateful to TV because it has given them an opportunity to live a normal family life" (Wolters 6, 25). An April 6, 1952, *L.A. Examiner* article ran a picture of the couple smooching in bed with the caption, "When Desi and Lucille do scenes like this in their TV show, they aren't just play-acting—they really mean it." Or as "a friend" of Ball's quipped in a June 1952 *Look* article, "The trouble with Lucy is that her real life is so much like her reel life" (Silvian 7).

Of course, despite the publicity's insistence that the series was based on the Ball and Arnaz marriage, clearly it was not. The Ricardos struggled financially and were renters of a one-bedroom apartment, not the owners of a ranch and production company like Ball and Arnaz. The Ricardos were childless (like *My Favorite Husband* characters), but Ball and Arnaz had a daughter. But most importantly, there is a huge yawning gap between the famous and talented celebrity Lucille Ball and the unknown, marginalized Lucy Ricardo, who yearns to be in the act but is stuck in the home. One way to think about the difference is that the series not only made it possible for Ball and Arnaz to be together and save their marriage (at least for the next ten years, until they divorced in 1959), but it also created a public fantasy of a private life in line with traditional gender ideals of postwar American culture.

The authorship and production contexts of *I Love Lucy* offer information about the "encoding" of the series—where ideas came from, how they were adapted from other sources like the radio show or the audience's knowledge about Ball and Arnaz's life, and how the creative team collaborated to author the character of Lucy. It took a group of men and women, some creative, some technical, and some financial, working on the series and the surrounding publicity to produce the Lucy phenomenon, to make Lucy TV. Operating within industrial, technical, and cultural limitations, they drew on their personal experiences, identity, and beliefs as well as on the traditions of narrative, comedy, and performance with which they were familiar in order to craft *I Love Lucy*'s fictional world and its inhabitants.

Narrative and Comedic Conventions and Innovations of the Situation Comedy

The Basics of Lucy TV

I Love Lucy made television history with its mode of production; it also made television history by establishing many audiovisual and narrative conventions for the television situation comedy, as we saw in the previous chapter. Of course, the stories were told visually and aurally, so it is hard to separate style and content, but this chapter focuses specifically on the narrative conventions and innovations of television situation comedy instituted at the beginning of the series, when the plots, themes, and characters were established and refined, and before the basic format shifted with the pregnancy and baby shows.

Like many television series, *I Love Lucy* has different phases: an initial, establishing period (the first half of the first season); a period when it hits its stride, deepening and refining the initial premise (second half of first season and the second season) and culminating in the pregnancy shows; a time when revisions are necessary to keep the series fresh (third through the first half of the sixth season), when the characters travel to Hollywood and Europe; and a self-conscious end period when the premise has shifted significantly from the original (halfway through the sixth season), when Lucy and Ricky leave New York City and move to Connecticut.[1] *I Love Lucy* also had a pre-series phase, and built on the solid foundation of the successful radio show *My Favorite Husband* (1948–51) to reinforce the conventions of the sitcom that were already established. In making the transition to television, the ideas expressed in the scripts were reinforced and extended by the visual style, economy of production, and secondary texts like magazine and newspaper articles.

Plots, Characters, and Comedy in *My Favorite Husband* and *I Love Lucy*

Even though Ball and Arnaz made the show their own in many ways, *I Love Lucy* was based on the narratives produced and written by the same talented *My Favorite Husband* team of Jess Oppenheimer, Madelyn Pugh, and Bob Carroll Jr. The radio show concerned the life of Liz and George Cugat. The tag line of the series was "Two people who live together . . . and like it!"[2] The show was based on the book *Mr. and Mrs. Cugat: The Record of a Happy Marriage,* by Isobel Scott Rorick, which focused on wealthy "society" people. However, Oppenheimer thought that audiences would be able to identify more closely with the characters if it was clear they were not well-off, and so when he came on board, the Cugats took a downwardly mobile turn and became the Coopers, with lack of money as a prime source of their conflicts. Oppenheimer also introduced another couple to act as foils for George and Liz. The most significant change Oppenheimer made to the character who evolved into Lucy was to make Liz more like Baby Snooks, the child protagonist (played by adult Broadway star Fanny Brice) of the hit radio show he wrote before moving to *My Favorite Husband.* Instead of being a sophisticate in an equal marriage like the original Liz Cugat, Oppenheimer made Liz a childish schemer whose comic exploits stemmed from getting her way from an initial position of inequality. If we still see traces of infantilization in Lucy Ricardo, this is its source. It is also the root of her trickery.

My Favorite Husband was broadcast live, like the majority

of radio shows, with commercial messages for the sponsors at the beginning, middle, and end. There was even a recipe using Jell-O that was read in the middle. As we saw in the previous chapter, doing the commercials for Jell-O during *My Favorite Husband* helped Ball develop many of the voices that later evolved into sounds, facial expressions, mannerisms, and characters that became fodder for various impersonations of Lucy Ricardo. Of course, Ball built on her success as a film comedienne, particularly in the late 1940s and into 1950 with *Fancy Pants* (1950), *The Fuller Brush Girl* (1950), and *Miss Grant Takes Richmond* (1949), all of which featured Ball doing slapstick comedy. But it was only in the recurring role of Liz, and then Lucy, that she was really able to develop her comedy. Oppenheimer encouraged her to ham it up for the audience, and after watching Jack Benny's radio broadcast, Ball understood how an interaction with the audience could translate even though the home listeners couldn't see her. That connection with the audience carried over to *I Love Lucy,* in part because of Oppenheimer's belief that people had to identify with the characters.

There are some noticeable differences between *My Favorite Husband* and *I Love Lucy.* The television episodes, even when they are based directly on a radio episode script, seem to take fewer risks in their verbal humor; they seem less adult oriented. Of course, there is no point of comparison for the visual comedy, although the narratives are often identical, and surprisingly, some of the most visual and physical *I Love Lucy* bits, like Lucy and Ricky handcuffed, Lucy with a beard and moustache, or the exploding rice in "Job Switching," originated in scripts for *My Favorite Husband.* Perhaps it was changing times, concern about the new medium, a different sponsor, or the influence of Ball and Arnaz's real-life marriage, but in many ways, Lucy is tamer than Liz was; the entire dynamic of the two marriages is different. Liz and George have a we-love-each-other-and-to-hell-with-everyone-else attitude that Ricky and Lucy never quite have; the Cugats/Coopers seem unconcerned with how the outside world sees them, perhaps because neither character is in the public eye the way that Ricky is and Lucy longs to be. George doesn't have the same temper as Ricky, so the power dynamic is different as well. Maybe some of the difference is between being heard and being seen.

Central Conflict/Source of Comedy in *I Love Lucy*

Comedy relies on conflict, on friction; the sitcom in particular sets up a structure of situation, disruption, and resolution/reinstatement of status quo. The pilot (then called an audition) for *I Love Lucy* set up one of the most characteristic tensions—and therefore sources of comedy—of the series: Lucy wants to be in the show, but Ricky doesn't want her to be. Here is the premise, in the words of the idea that producer Jess Oppenheimer registered with the Screen Writer's Guild:

> He is a Latin-American orchestra leader and singer. She is his wife. They are happily married and very much in love. The only bone of contention between them is her desire to get into show business, and his equally strong desire to keep her out of it. To Lucy . . . show business is the most glamorous field in the world. But Ricky, who was raised in show business, sees none of its glamour, only its deficiencies, and yearns to be an ordinary citizen. . . . The closest he can get to this dream is having a wife who's out of show business and devotes herself to keeping as nearly normal a life as possible for him.
>
> The first story concerns a TV audition for Ricky, where Pepito, the clown, due to an accident, fails to appear and Lucy takes his place for the show. Although she does a bang-up job, she foregoes the chance at a career that is offered to her in order to keep Ricky happy and closer to his dream of normalcy. (*Laughs* 139)

The sexism of the premise and the producer's affinity for Ricky's masculine point of view leap off the page, reflecting the domestic ideology of the cold war era, which idealized gender differences and the wife's supporting, unequal role. Oppenheimer's description makes it seem like the show should have been called "I Love Ricky!" Of course, many observers from biographers to media historians and critics have noted that Ball and Arnaz actively pursued an alternative fiction in the series in which the husband was more famous, and nothing ended up in the show if Ball and Arnaz didn't approve.

The pilot did not include other characters, except for the clown whom Lucy replaces and Ricky's agent; it was when the creators got the go-ahead to make a series that Fred and Ethel Mertz were created to fulfill a similar function as Iris and Rudolph Atterbury, the older, wealthier couple on *My Favorite Husband*, Liz's best friend and George's friend and boss. Ethel also took on some of the function of Liz's maid, Kate, as a sounding board and co-conspirator. With minimal changes, entire scenes of dialogue could be lifted from the radio scripts, and twenty-one of the first season's thirty-five episodes were based in part or entirely on *My Favorite Husband* scripts.

The writers had fixed ideas about the structure and scope of each show—that they be rooted in common experience, built logically, and as Madelyn Pugh Davis recalled in her autobiography, end on a positive note because Ball "said each show should end happily." "In coming up with ideas for the show, we always tried to start with a universal theme, something the audience could identify with and nod and say, 'That same thing happened to me.' Sometimes when we were looking for a new story line, Bob would say, 'What'll we do this week? Jealousy? Greed? Envy? The men versus the women? Money?'" (86, 87).

I Love Lucy brought together four central characters that were written to play to the strengths of the actors who portrayed them. The writers knew Lucille Ball from *My Favorite Husband* and developed the series specifically for her and Desi

Arnaz, whom they also knew. The other two main characters on the show, Ethel and Fred Mertz, played by Vivian Vance and William Frawley, did not get along on a personal level, and that friction also became part of the characters' dynamic. The comic conflicts shifted so that sometimes it split the four characters along gender lines and sometimes along generational lines, with the older and younger couple having and resolving a conflict. The depth of the characters, created by the interplay of the excellent writing and acting, allows for seemingly endless interpersonal interaction, and is largely responsible for how well the series holds up over time.

It is interesting that the plot device that people remember most—Lucy trying to get into Ricky's show—actually was not the most commonly used plot. Although it was the initial premise for the pilot, in the first season about as many episodes revolved around marriage and domesticity (fifteen) as focused on show business (fourteen), with six shows on the battle of the sexes and one about a Mertz versus Ricardo fight. Perhaps propelled by the narrative shift to the pregnancy and baby shows, in the second and third seasons, however, there are far more shows concerning domesticity and marriage than Lucy trying to get into show business (nineteen versus five in season two and twenty-one versus six in season three). Other plot devices that are repeated through the first three seasons are battle-of-the-sexes plots, which pit the men against the women (six in the first season, four in the second, and three in the third) and feuds between the Ricardos and the Mertzes (five in all three seasons combined). So, although the stories of Lucy crashing Ricky's show may have been foundational and most memorable, the series as a whole had a primarily domestic focus, and even the show business episodes emphasize the Ricardo's home life, often beginning and ending in the home, with scenes in Ricky's club in the middle.

It is also interesting that this plot device, Lucy literally trying to break into the middle of Ricky's live act, became a series trope because of a restriction. In the initial series contract, advertising executive Milton Biow included a clause in the contract with Desilu that restricted Arnaz's singing: "It is agreed that in each program the major emphasis shall be placed on the basic situations arising out of the fictional marriage of [Lucy and Ricky Ricardo], and that the orchestra will furnish only incidental or background music except where an *occasional* script shall *require* a vocal number by Desi Arnaz *as part of the story line*" (qtd. in Oppenheimer, *Laughs* 173). Oppenheimer recalls that in order to comply with the contract, the writers wrote scenes in which Ricky was in the middle of a performance and Lucy's trademark comic disruption, publicly upstaging and destroying the structure and constraints of "the act," was born. The contract was changed after the show became a hit, and perhaps that explains why that plot is used less frequently.

43

Sitcom Structure

As we have seen, the original first-season viewers of *I Love Lucy* already knew many of the conventions of the television situation comedy because they were familiar with the characters, plots, dialogue, themes, jokes, conflicts, resolutions, settings, and the ways time and space were organized from radio sitcoms. In other words, the situation comedy already existed on paper and in the audience's ear and "radio eye"—a 1920s RCA advertisement's term. Moreover, many radio programs were based on comic strips that ran in newspapers and had visual publicity materials that helped shape images for the audiences to complement the words, sounds, and music of the radio programs. Of course, the new television audience also brought experience in film spectatorship, which cinematographer Karl Freund, editor Danny Cahn, and director Marc Daniels brought to their visual interpretation of the scripts. Nevertheless, the new amalgamation of visual comedy, the half-hour time frame divided by a commercial in the middle, the practices of television watching in the home, and the production system of filming before a live studio audience created something new: the genre of television situation comedy.

Genre is an understanding between the industry and the audience; it is a grouping of individual texts by a common set of narrative conventions, iconography, characters, audiovisual style, and themes. There are different ways to define genre, but what matters here for our discussion of *I Love Lucy*'s role in the development of the television situation comedy genre is that genre sets up expectations that must both remain stable and also enough that the show does not become boring. In "Fictions and Ideologies: The Case of Situation Comedy," Janet Woollacott draws on earlier work about how the narrative of situation comedy is based on a dichotomy of inside/outside to suggest that "the tension of the narrative to which the viewer responds revolves around the economy or wit with which the two discourses [of inside and outside, or home and work] are brought together in the narrative. The pleasure of situation comedy is linked to the release of that tension through laughter" (171). Woollacott's 1986 analysis provides a framework for attention to the *structure* of the sitcom by highlighting the *dichotomy* at the center of the conflict-driven plots (which evolves into the multiple narrative threads of the postmodern situation comedy "about nothing," *Seinfeld*), and also how the *pleasure* of the sitcom is achieved through the familiar viewer's appreciation of the comic efficiency with which the narrative resolves the conflict, not whether it is resolved.

To be sure, the enjoyment in watching *I Love Lucy* comes from the comedy, from the carefully structured buildup to a comic climax so brilliantly performed by Lucille Ball and her costars. Everything else is the setup—ideologically revealing, but setup nevertheless. As critic Patricia Mellencamp argues, "if Lucy's plots for ambition and fame narratively failed . . . performatively they succeeded" (88). We want Lucy to fail because that is what's funny, although there is also great humor in

Lucy and Ethel's domestic experience conflicts with the world of work in "Job Switching."

her moments of triumph. Moreover, the situation of the sitcom dictates her failure in individual episodes. We know that Lucy will not be made costar in Ricky's act, or have her own career, or somehow resolve the conflict Ricky and Lucy have over what Lucy's proper place is. But what we don't know is precisely *how* she will manage to botch it this time.

The contradiction of Lucy "failing" so Ball and the series can succeed hinged on Ball's uncanny ability to achieve *sprezzatura*, the Italian term for "the art that conceals art, the supremely artificial that strikes us as supremely natural" (Mast 26). It is the illusion of spontaneity at which Ball excelled; every account of the series' production recalls the long hours of rehearsal that

Ball put in as she interpreted what the writers called THE BLACK STUFF, the stage directions written in capital letters, that detailed the comic bits that Lucy made look so artless and unplanned. There were moments of improvisation, but few, and usually Ball riffed on what was already a solidly written bit, like in the famous scene in "L.A. at Last!" (February 7, 1955, with actor William Holden) when her false nose catches fire. Although it was said that Ball improvised putting out her flaming putty nose in the coffee cup, it was actually written that she take off the fake nose and put it out. Instead she dipped her head so the nose goes in the cup. It is a small shift, but it is comic genius. Even when the jig is up and William Holden will know she is the woman who dumped food on him in the restaurant, Lucy is still trying to maintain her disguise, trying to get away with it. One of my first memories of Lucy is my mother laughing so hard at that. Like many people, including Ball, it is her favorite Lucy moment.

The Example of "Job Switching"

The episode "Job Switching" fits what writer Madelyn Pugh Davis explained was the typical structure of an episode, with a smaller physical bit for Lucy in the first half and the entire episode leading up to a comic climax. In that episode, the earlier bit is when Lucy is alone with the "real" chocolate dipper; the comedy plays off of the contrast between the person who knows what she is doing and the one who does not. In the second physical bit, Lucy and Ethel are placed together at the conveyor belt, and again there is the contrast between Lucy and someone else who highlights her incredible physical prowess and facility with props. She is *very* fast at wrapping the chocolates, but not as fast as the machine dictates. In standard Lucy fashion, optimism and the hope that she is faking it convincingly only gets her so far, and this time it prompts the supervisor to call out, "Speed it up a little!"

Together, Lucy and Ethel are funnier than Lucy alone in "Job Switching."

The conveyor belt bit was certainly not new; Charlie Chaplin in *Modern Times* (1936) comes to mind, and in that film, we see a critique of how working on an assembly line makes a person machinelike. This fits nicely with Henri Bergson's theory that comedy stems from "something mechanical encrusted on the living," and Ball and Vance's interaction with the machine, their clash between the living and the mechanical, is underscored comically by their nonprofessional, organic, nonmechanical reaction of trying to eat or hide the chocolates that get by them. From the beginning of the episode, the women are out of their element, the home, and thrust into the world of paid work in which they have no experience or skills. That Lucy tries to fake it is hilarious; that Lucy and Ethel try to fake it *together* puts it over the top. By building from Lucy's individual bit with the professional candy dipper to the comic duet with Ethel, the comedic stakes rise. Visually, we have two different rhythms as the belt speeds up, which is funnier than one, but most importantly, here are Lucy and Ethel, in a crazy situation *again*.

The series helped to establish a narrative structure that defined the conventions of the situation comedy. In "Job Switching" we can see that the story has three parts: the setup, ending with an inciting incident; the second act that builds to a comic climax; and the denouement/resolution. The episode begins in the Ricardo living room, as the majority of episodes do, then moves out to the world beyond the home, and returns to it at the end. The story of this particular episode echoes the structure, because it involves Lucy and Ethel getting jobs outside of the home, culminating in the famous conveyor belt scene at the chocolate factory. Pugh recalls, "Jess and Bob and I were working out the story line for the script, and we wanted a funny job for Lucy and Ethel to end up doing, so we got out the phone book and looked in the *Yellow Pages*. When we got to 'C,' we said, 'Aha! Candy making!' Then Bob and I went to the Farmer's Market and watched a woman dipping chocolates to see how she did it" (Davis 71).

Each scene builds to a comic conflict, reinforcing the status quo disruption-resolution plot. Here is a breakdown of the scenes in "Job Switching," with the plot elements, set, and comic devices indicated.

Scene 1: *Ricardo living room:* Ricky and Lucy argue about money. They are joined by Fred and Ethel and the conversation turns to a battle-of-the-sexes challenge: Ricky and Fred will do the housework and the "girls" will go out and get paid jobs. This scene relies on comic dialogue.

Scene 2: *Ricardo kitchen:* Ricky and Lucy switch gender roles at breakfast, with Lucy reading the paper, Ricky trying to get her attention, and Ricky providing the breakfast. Then Lucy finds out Ricky has ordered the breakfast, not cooked it himself. This scene uses dialogue and props.

Scene 3: *Employment office:* Lucy and Ethel go to the employment office, but they don't have any employable skills or experience. This scene employs dialogue, and facial expressions/ pantomime.

Scene 4: *Ricardo living room:* Ricky, in an apron, and Fred, in a headscarf, botch the housework, even as they believe they are doing a good job. This scene uses comic props and dialogue.

Scene 5: *Candy factory:* At the candy factory, Lucy is assigned to chocolate dipping. This scene is the first of the physical comedy pieces in the episode, and also uses dialogue and props to build to the slapstick slapping between Lucy and the candy dipper.

Scene 6: *Ricardo living room and kitchen:* Ricky and Fred show off their domestic abilities to each other, moving into the kitchen for a comic scene that culminates in the broad physical comedy of Ricky and Fred trying to contain the four pounds of rice that overflow the pot on the stove. This slapstick scene, with the chickens bursting out of the pressure cooker, the rice oozing all over the kitchen, and Ricky falling down in it, mirrors the physical intensification in the previous scene and anticipates the shift from confidence to calamity that escalates in the next scene. It was based on a scene from *My Favorite Husband,* including the brilliant comic exchange:

RICKY: Do you know anything about rice?
FRED: I know it was thrown at me on one of the darkest days of my life.

Scene 7: *Candy factory:* Ethel and Lucy are moved to the conveyor belt, after failing in other departments of the candy factory. This scene also builds in intensity as the chocolates they are supposed to wrap move faster and faster on the belt, and they stuff them into their hats, shirts, and mouths in their effort not to let one candy get past them unwrapped. Physical comedy and props are used here in a classic comedic setup pitting human against machine that starts under control and then escalates. Ball's physical ability is showcased again here with her swift hand movements.

Scene 8: *Ricardo living room:* The girls return to the Ricardo apartment, where they see the horrible mess in the kitchen and the men and women decide to go back to their normal gender roles. "We never realized how tough it was to run a house before," Ricky concedes, and to show their appreciation, the men give the women, of all things, boxes of chocolates. In this concluding scene, which provides the happy ending on which Ball insisted, there is a return to dialogue and props, and a quieter, slower tone.

Breaking down the episode in this way shows us several aspects of the structure of the sitcom form in its infancy. First, we can recognize the efficient production design at work with only a few sets and characters. Second, we can see the way that Woollacott's inside/outside dichotomy provides an organizing principle for plot, characters, and themes. Third, we can appreciate the escalation of comic outlandishness at the same time that the writers maintain a consistent internal logic and cause and effect; this is where the pleasure of the sitcom comes from. It all makes sense within the world the writers have created, Lucy's world. Fourth, we can appreciate the deployment of the different techniques of comedy at different times in each scene and throughout the episode, such as dialogue, props, slapstick, pantomime, costume and makeup, and physical comedy.

As Oppenheimer recalled, the physical comedy, the props, and comic antics would only work if the audience knew there was a logical reason for each development. "I knew from experience that if you start with a believable premise and take the audience one step at a time, and they know why they're being taken there, you can go to the heights of slapstick comedy and outlandish situations." He notes that because the conveyor belt speeds up for a reason—the supervisor thinks they are doing a good job because she doesn't realize what the women have done with the chocolates—the scene doesn't "violate the logic of the moment" (*Laughs* 186, 187). In each of the scenes, in each of the parallel lines of action, and in the episode's narrative as a whole, there is the buildup of tension between the abilities and expectations of the characters on the one hand and the demands of the situation in which they find themselves on the other; all of this originates in the logical premise of the situation and our knowledge of the characters.

In "Job Switching" and other episodes from the first two seasons, we can see that there were many aspects of theater, film, and radio comedy in play: comedic narrative structure as outlined above, the use of comic props, costumes, physical comedy, and verbal comedy. The feminine items like the apron and headscarf that the men wear, or the candy maker hats that Lucy and Ethel wear contribute to the comic effect and work as a comic shorthand. In many episodes, Fred walks into the Ricardo apartment and gets a laugh because of his costume (and deadpan expression). Lucy employs a range of costumes as disguises in her schemes; hair and makeup are often involved as well. The props that were used in "Job Switching" range from the starched stocking and flat cake that Fred bakes, to the chocolate that Lucy hilariously fails to wrap, to the frothing rice that flows like volcanic lava all over the Ricardo kitchen.

Ultimately, the laughs in "Job Switching" emanate not only from the comic bits but also from the reflection of society, and in particular of the ideal and real economic relations of the sexes in marriage, that is created in the episode. At a time when the domestic ideology romanticized married women as happy homemakers who didn't need or want to work outside the home, "Job Switching" depicted both women's desire for financial independence and also anxiety about the skills needed to get work (complicated of course by it being Lucy). The men's experience doing housework gives them a new appreciation for "women's work" as actual work. In many ways, this episode typifies a sitcom "resolution": nothing has *really* changed, the inside is back on the inside and the outside is outside again, the women and men will go back to where they "belong," but with some new kind of understanding . . . that will be gone by next week's episode.

Conclusion

Ball's brilliance at physical comedy, and the excellent slapstick abilities of her costars, gave *I Love Lucy* something that few sitcoms have had. Coupled with funny writing that resonated culturally with the home- and family-focused postwar audience, the comic climaxes were and remain deeply funny. In both the conveyor belt and kitchen fiascos, the situation is beyond the character's control, but the person valiantly continues to do the best they can, resulting in greater and greater silliness—a specialty of Ball's from her film days on. Ball's comic embodiment of Lucy—with all her ambition, pluck, unshakable optimism, and inventiveness—makes use of every gesture, every movement, every expression, and every line of dialogue. The characters, their patterns of interaction, and the narrative expectations that *I Love Lucy* pioneered provide not only the context for the deepening of those characters throughout the series but for the genre of situation comedy itself.

Trickster Lucy

Popularity, Comedy, Gender, and Culture

As we have seen, *I Love Lucy* emerged out of a production context of early television and within the framework established on radio, but the Lucy phenomenon—her popularity, influence, and longevity—went beyond television. The combination of culturally resonant themes, superior comedy writing, and Lucille Ball's unprecedented physical comedy made history. When you picture Lucy, perhaps you see her at the height of one of her schemes, one of her many escape attempts from the confines of domesticity. Maybe you recall her trademark red hair (which was well known despite the series being in black and white), her big eyes looking from side to side to see if she has been caught, her valiant smile trying to project success when there has been yet another failure. Lucy became an American icon who embodied endless optimism and boundless creativity, a new kind of comic heroine built on the legacy of madcaps, screwballs, and con women, shaped by the traditions of film and stage physical comedy, bristling against 1950s domestic ideology.

Part of the reason why *I Love Lucy* was so phenomenally popular is that it incorporated a beloved character—the trickster—updating and reinventing it in what emerged as a central story cycle in postwar American culture in the new medium of television. Unlike the conventional hero who achieves his goal through strength, power, and hard work, the trickster is shifty and clever, and gets what he or she wants through deception, tricks, and rule breaking.[1] The trickster dons disguises, plays roles, crosses gender and class, causes trouble, and stirs up the status quo. In some cultures, the trickster is a little animal, like the coyote in Southwest Native American traditions that bests creatures who are bigger and stronger through his or her wiliness, and sometimes the trickster's mischief backfires and he or she is the dupe. By uniting the most lofty and the most base of human characteristics, the trickster figure performs the cultural work of fusing binary oppositions, like sacred and profane, or masculine and feminine. In popular culture, the trickster most often appears in the genre of comedy, although some con artists and shape-shifters emerge in drama as well.

By thinking of Lucy as a trickster, our focus shifts from the specifics of television situation comedy in the 1950s and takes a broader, more anthropological, view of how stories and characters function in human cultures. Considering Lucy as a trickster alongside other animal and human trickster figures, like Br'er Rabbit, Anansi the Spider, Hermes, the leprechaun, the lutin, Maui, Raven, and Monkey, makes a leap from premodern, oral folklore to modern, audiovisual, recorded culture, and there certainly are important distinctions to be made. It sheds light on American culture in the 1950s to view Lucy as a trickster in the new terrain of television, crossing the boundaries between public and private spheres, reality and artifice, and masculine and feminine behaviors.[2]

Moreover, thinking of Lucy as a specifically *female* trickster who employs the tactics of deception, impersonation, and trickery to slip out of Ricky's control helps us see the character in a context even wider than postwar American culture, and helps explain Lucy's appeal. The physical comedy for which Ball is so justly remembered stems narratively from Lucy's trickster energy, her refusal to accept things the way they are, and her rejection of limitations society or her husband impose. As a trickster, she performs the cultural work of calling attention to the boundaries between social spaces (like home and the world), categories (public and private), and roles (housewife and professional or masculine and feminine) that the culture sets up as oppositional. A trickster creates a new possibility when faced with two choices, a third way out that reimagines the situation. Of course, the trickster's schemes often backfire and the trickster is the dupe, because society is not so elastic as to allow for the trickster's remaking of social roles, metaphors, practices, and spaces.

Lucy is specifically a female trickster because she portrays the paradox of the "feminine mystique," to use Betty Friedan's term for the postwar representation of women as both powerful and ineffective. Female trickery is necessitated by women's subordinate position; if women are not stronger or more powerful than men, they must resort to covert rather than overt tactics to achieve their goals. If Ricky controls the money, and decides Lucy can't have what she wants, then Lucy must create a situation in which she can gain access to the money through trickery. In addition, by using conventionally female tactics like makeup, emotional manipulation, and sex appeal in addition to the trickster tactics of disguise, parody, feigned submission, impersonation, and deception, Lucy highlights the inconsistencies of the sex-gender system.

In portraying marriage as a situation that necessitated female trickery, *I Love Lucy* presented both a conventional, mainstream view of marriage and also a protofeminist challenge to it. The mainstream, dominant ideology of postwar domesticity was that married women should not have jobs; of course, this is a highly class-biased view, because many working-class women have always worked, whether they were married or not. Nevertheless, this is one of the residual ideas about women's roles that was challenged by women's participation in the workforce during World War II and never went away, although the dominant cultural discourses tried to act as if it did. So, the ideal situation portrayed in *I Love Lucy* is Lucy without a job, dependent on Ricky for money and responsible only for the home. However, the series also enacted the actors' vanguard perspective that women should have careers after marriage, a point of view that was emergent in the 1950s but not yet mainstream, just by Ball's participation in the public sphere as an actress and star. Of course, Ball and Arnaz, and the writers, including Madelyn Pugh, one of the few women television writers in the era, grounded their work in their experiences of gender in the postwar era, surrounded by the same domestic revival as any other American, yet distinct from it as part of Hollywood's more egalitarian culture.

When we examine many episodes from the series, we can see that when Lucy uses female trickery to preserve her autonomy in the home, she is successful, but when she tries to go outside her "place" in the domestic sphere, there is a sharp boomerang and she lands right back where she started. This is an example of how a representation of female trickery exposes the cultural tensions between the limitations of femininity and women's aspirations. A character like Lucy stretches the boundaries, if at first only of representation, but then also of the imagination. Perhaps the best example of how female trickery works within the domestic sphere is the episode "Lucy's Schedule" (May 26, 1952, based on an April 22, 1949, *My Favorite Husband* script). When Ricky decides to put Lucy on a schedule because he is tired of her inability to manage her time, Lucy conspires with Ethel and the wife of Ricky's boss on a trick to make their husbands reject the schedule. Lucy's trickery works because she is trying to regain control over how she does her work in the domestic sphere; the episode reinforces cultural ideals about separate spheres for men and women.[3]

In her film career, Ball struggled to position herself within the contradictions of femininity. When she abandoned her bleached blond look and went red in the mid-1930s, she rejected the gold digger/dumb blond "type" and located herself as the unconventional, vivacious, and screwball redhead first mythologized by 1920s "titian" celebrity writer and film producer "Madame" Elinor Glyn in her collaboration with famous redhead Clara Bow on two hit movies of the Jazz Age: *It* (1927) and *Red Hair* (1928), which associated individuality and self-confidence with red-haired women. The wisecracking screwball characters that Ball played before Lucy, including Liz on *My Favorite Husband,* walked a fine line between feminine and unfeminine when the comedy became physical, something that "Beauty into Buffoon," the title of a 1952 *Life* magazine article, indicates, seemed like a strange choice for a beautiful woman. Indeed, many of Lucy's funniest bits played on the antithesis of ideal housewife femininity in what she wore (men's clothes, baggy clothes, messy clothes, too-tight clothes); how she moved her body (out of control, clumsily, selfishly); and what motivated her behavior (desire for fame, public recognition, self-actualization).

Ball located herself in the tradition of screwball heroines who had developed on radio and in comic strips alongside film, but in shifting media from film to radio to television, and in more conservative times, grew increasingly domesticated. It is hard to imagine any of screwball comedy's best heroines, like *Bringing Up Baby*'s Susan Vance, played by Katherine Hepburn, living out their lives in domesticity, and indeed that was the concept for *My Favorite Husband* before Oppenheimer transformed it. That lingering issue of what happens to the screwball when she marries and becomes a wife was a particularly pertinent one for postwar American culture. The screwball that emerges from the discourses of women's liberation in the Jazz Age, reinterpreted by Hollywood in the Depression, takes on a very different tone in the "homeward bound" 1950s.

When Lucy Ricardo inherits the legacy of the screwball heroine, it is indeed in a new, domestic situation that is repeated weekly. Because Lucy can't satisfy her desires in a straightforward way, she uses trickery. Because of her status as a married woman and her lack of economic autonomy, it is often her husband's authority she is trying to subvert by employing the covert tactics of "feminine wiles" that are open to her. This topic could not have been as successful in a drama, but comedy allowed a playful exploration of the social boundaries of the time. The gap between the ideals of polarized gender roles and the reality of the social experience of men and women was significant in the postwar era, and the irreconcilable clash between Lucy's ambitions and her social position as wife and mother spoke to sharpening tensions in American culture. As a trickster in the central postwar story cycle of *I Love Lucy*, Lucy exposed the boundaries of socially accepted gender roles, appropriate middle-class behavior, and where self-motivation and womanly selflessness clash. Her failures to escape domesticity sketch a comic map of the contested terrain of postwar America.

Lucy embodies the culture's contradictory ideas about women's relationships to both domestic and nondomestic pursuits. She wants to be a good wife, and then mother, but she also wants to participate in the world outside the home. The show hedges its ideological bets by making Lucy's singing, dancing, and performing talents limited, so it is not only Ricky's desire for his wife to be "just a wife" (to quote the pilot episode) that keeps Lucy in the home. By replaying Lucy's desire to escape domesticity over and over again, the desire gets the emphasis.

Female Friendship

The male trickster is most often a solitary figure, but the female trickster who emerges in twentieth-century American popular culture often has a female friend, a sidekick, less zany than she, but nevertheless willing to go along for the ride. One of the most enduring aspects of *I Love Lucy* (and one necessary to the continuation of the Lucy character after the end of the original series, when Ball and Vance's friendship outlasted the Ball-Arnaz marriage) is the friendship between Lucy and Ethel. This is a remarkable portrayal of female friendship, one that is not idealized (they have fights, jealousies, and rivalries), but rings true in that Ethel will do anything, *anything,* to help out her friend, even when she knows it is a crazy idea. Lucy alone of course is funny, but the two of them together are funnier.

As actresses and collaborators, Lucille Ball and Vivian Vance shared remarkable chemistry and timing. Vance explained her relationship with Ball: "She and I were just like sisters. We fought like sisters and made up the same way. We shared a rare sense of balance, Lucille and I, much like the instinct of a diver who judges precisely the right moment to leave the springboard. . . . We could take off together, singing or dancing, matching the notes and the steps, without having to think about it" (qtd. in Castelluccio and Walker 199). In the same way that the writers based the on-screen relationship between Lucy and Ricky on elements of the actors' personalities and relationship, they were able to build on the real-life friendship and collaboration between Ball and Vance, and so we have an example of two women working closely together, as a team, with their conflicts and reconciliations only deepening their emotional bond.

Although Vivian Vance was considered the best "second banana in the business," and the character of Ethel a terrific foil, the relationship between the two is mutual. Sometimes Ethel plays the role of the older, more experienced woman, but she is usually sucked into Lucy's tricky optimism, which keeps her from turning cynical. Lucy lifts Ethel beyond the dullness of everyday life; Ethel is always just one moment of cajoling away from doing something crazy that she wants to do but wouldn't instigate. Of course, Lucy needs Ethel for company and backup, but when we stop and think about it, it is clear that she needs Ethel for much more. It is with Ethel, not Ricky, that Lucy can truly be herself; she does not have to scheme and impersonate to interact with Ethel in a satisfying way. Perhaps that is the essence of female friendship, of best friendship, that Lucy and Ethel embody so compellingly. Recently, a rerun of *I Love Lucy* aired on Nick at Nite's TV Land cable channel right before a showing of the film *Thelma and Louise* (1991); this struck me as a fitting pairing. Although Thelma and Louise's exploits certainly do not occur within the safe, comic world of the sitcom, the emotional resonance of the intimacy and interdependence of the two women stepping outside the confines of conventional femininity, turning to trickery, is similar to that created in the relationship between Lucy and Ethel. In a way, Thelma and Louise are tragic extensions of Lucy and Ethel, ripped out of the sitcom world, propelled through the desert, hands clasped defiantly in a world that has no place for them. The comic containment of the sitcom world that rocks Lucy and Ethel back into domesticity, back into their marriages (a better bet for Lucy than Ethel) also makes room for zany comic possibilities for a pair of female tricksters to, for example, impersonate Martian women, or don a host of other disguises closer to home.

Ultimately, Lucy can be Lucy—with her unquenchable ambition and her unfazed optimism that *this* time, her scheme will work—because she has Ethel as her friend. Every time Ethel looks at Lucy with disbelief, it makes Lucy's plan funnier. Every time Ethel ends up helping Lucy anyway, it makes it funnier. And it speaks powerfully to the idea of female friendship, in which neither is afraid to be wrong, look stupid, or fail, and when she inevitably does, the other supports her anyway. They are in it together, not alone. The "I" in the title *I Love Lucy* may have been Desi Arnaz, but it is also Ethel, and Lucy's intense relationship with Ethel suggests that the female trickster does not have to be a solitary figure, committed to independence over intimacy, like the male trickster so often is.

Female trickery is not solitary in "Lucy Is Envious."

The Trick of Commercial Television: Commodifying the Trickster

The show's producers, sponsor, and network also needed Lucy to "fail" so that the situation persisted and *I Love Lucy* could continue; this is one of the tricks of a television series, especially a situation comedy. Although the text of *I Love Lucy* is fascinating for how it reflected and shaped American culture, the real purpose of the show was to make money, to become a commodity, and in this, it redefined success in the postwar era. Commodification is a process of transforming experience, ideas, and senses of self into the quantifiable products of consumer culture, and placing those products in a social context in which people define things in terms of themselves and themselves in terms of things so that "self" is created and understood through the goods and appearance of the goods people consume. Cultural representations and social practices reinforce the idea that the commodities a person consumes and displays are the source of a person's character and worth, not anything intrinsic or internal. The Lucy phenomenon of Lucy TV—the television series, the "Lucy" merchandise, the publicity, the secondary texts, and the character—are all part of one of the most successful products television and postwar American society has ever made.

An advertisement that exclaimed, "Live Like Lucy!" indicates how *I Love Lucy* "tie-ups" embodied a lifestyle that television promoted. The Lucy and Ricky items included his and her pajamas (just like you see Ricky and Lucy wear), jewelry sets, aprons, dolls, comic books, diaper bags, Ricky smoking jackets, and furniture for every room.[4] In her autobiography, Ball recalled: "it was possible to furnish a house and dress a whole family with items carrying our *I Love Lucy* label. Red Skelton did a hilarious TV skit poking fun at this. As he walked into his house, his wife shouted, 'Don't track mud on my *I Love Lucy* rug!' As he started to sink into a chair, she added, 'Don't mess up my *I Love Lucy* chair!' He finally shoots her, and she moans, 'You shot a bullet through my *I Love Lucy* blouse!'" (224).

The ideal of domesticity that Lucy and Ricky enacted was indeed a commodified one, and many episodes revolved around a power struggle prompted by a consumer item like a new dress, furniture, a hat, or perhaps most hilariously, "The Freezer." Many episodes concern Lucy wanting to make money to buy something, or to make up for money she has already spent that she didn't have Ricky's permission to spend. By making mass consumer culture seem normal and funny, *I Love Lucy* performed the cultural work of the postwar era; by showing that culture not to ever be fully satisfying, it also performed the cultural work of critiquing the dominant culture. As we saw in the first chapter in the analysis of "Lucy Does a TV Commercial" and "Mr. and Mrs. TV Show," Lucy TV both enacted and

Lucy lets us in on the trick in "Lucy Makes a Television Commercial."

revealed how television is a trick, masquerading as entertainment and information, but really a vehicle for commercials.

This is fitting cultural work for a trickster to perform. As anthropologist Robert Pelton writes in *The Trickster in West Africa:* "The trickster violates boundaries to humanize them, but the 'new' shape that the world assumes is its present one. This is one of the points of the trickster's irony: all that wheeling and dealing, that endless juggling, simply keeps new balls flying through the air in the same order and at the same speed. . . . His transforming power has worked in the past to create the present, and it works in the present to make the future reflect the past. He moves past society's circumference to ensure the permanent rediscovery of its center" (248).

And, as we'll see in the next chapter, at the center of 1950s American society was trickster Lucy and Lucy TV.

A Spotlight on 1953

Lucy TV in Its Cultural Context

So far, we have looked at the origins of *I Love Lucy* in the wider context of 1950s television, as shaped by traditions and conventions of other cultural forms (radio, theater, film); its production context; the swirl of publicity that gave audiences extratextual information with which to decode the series and its secondary texts, like magazine and newspaper articles, advertisements, and commodities; and the audiovisual and narrative conventions the series established. We have also dipped our toes into the vast ocean of 1950s American culture—maybe splashed around in its ideology of postwar domesticity—but now we will dive into an exploration of Lucy TV in its cultural context, the height of the Lucy phenomenon: 1953.

By the end of its first season in 1951–52, *I Love Lucy* had skyrocketed to the top of the ratings charts. Lucy TV played a prominent role as more Americans bought televisions and made television-watching part of their lives. In the spring of 1952, the major national magazines like *Newsweek, Time, Look, Life,* and of course *TV Guide,* as well as many newspapers featured cover stories on the series and its stars. But the meteoric rise to new heights of cultural frenzy was yet to come, when *I Love Lucy* was caught up in the "baby boom," one of the cultural waves that defined the 1950s, with the simultaneous pregnancies of Lucille Ball and Lucy Ricardo.

Of course, as this book has argued, the Lucy phenomenon was thoroughly intertwined with cultural discourses of its time. That is why it was so popular: without being tautological, it resonated, struck a chord deep within the collective cultural psyche of mainstream American television viewers, reflecting and shaping the concerns of those who became participants in television culture. It set up the expectations of the style and content of television at the same time that it participated in popular discourse about social issues like gender, marriage, family, middle-class values, the baby boom, American identity, the desire for home ownership, and community.

This chapter explores three cultural currents in the metaphoric ocean of 1950s America. The first, the baby boom, is easy to see in all aspects of Lucy TV and in the broader culture, too. The second, discourses of ethnicity and race, specifically as they are expressed through music and performance, is there when you look, and sometimes you have to look more closely, because it is a deep current, sometimes played off superficially in *I Love Lucy*, but with a dangerous riptide simmering beneath. The third, the anticommunist blacklist and "red scare" also made for treacherous waters. Although it was certainly never mentioned in *I Love Lucy*, it threatened Lucy TV when Lucille Ball made headlines for being investigated as a suspected Communist by the House Un-American Activities Committee (HUAC). All three currents relate to what historian Elaine Tyler May calls the "two sides of the same coin" of "cold war ideology and the domestic revival" (10).

Baby Boom

When *I Love Lucy* was conceived, the Ricardos were childless, even though Ball was actually pregnant when they filmed the audition (now called a pilot) for the series. It was a show about marriage and domestic life, but not about a nuclear family. When, in the spring of their triumphant first season of their top-rated hit show, Ball and Arnaz realized they were expecting a second baby, they were thrilled like the millions of other Americans making the baby boom go boom, but also apprehensive. They finally had what they wanted for so long: both of their careers were successful and their work no longer kept them apart, their production company Desilu was growing rapidly, and a second baby was on the way when, at forty-one, Ball wasn't sure she would be able to have another. But no one had ever dealt directly with pregnancy on a hit television show before. Would their personal happiness mean the end of *I Love Lucy*?

It is hard to imagine in these times when pregnant stars pose seminude for the covers of magazines and there is endless speculation and study of celebrity women's possible baby bumps, but in the 1950s, pregnancy, including even uttering the word "pregnant" never mind showing a pregnant woman's body, was considered indelicate and not part of polite public discourse. In an excellent example of the gap between people's lived experience and cultural representation, although there were millions of pregnant women during the "baby boom," they were not depicted on television. Powerful cultural taboos against pregnancy that were "connected not only with the embarrassment inspired by visible signs of female sexual activity, but also with the fact that the pregnant body acts as both a reminder of our material origins and a signifier of the (uncertain) future" came into play (Hanson 14). Ball, Arnaz, producer Oppenheimer, and eventually CBS, the advertising agency, and the sponsor all took a risk and incorporated Ball's pregnancy into the series, riding the cultural wave of the baby boom to new heights of popularity and cultural resonance.

The baby boom was one of the factors that made Americans "homeward bound," to use May's term for the double-edged impulse toward and limitation within domesticity that char-

67

acterized the post–World War II generation. From the mid-1940s into the 1960s, more Americans married younger, had more children, and divorced less than at other times during the twentieth century. As May suggests in her study of cold war era families, there was a profound connection between private life and the wider cultural contexts; Americans created "a family-centered culture that was more than the internal reverberations of foreign policy, and went beyond the explicit manifestations of anticommunist hysteria such as McCarthyism and the 'Red Scare.' It took shape amid the legacy of the Depression, World War II, and the anxieties surrounding atomic weapons. It reflected the fears as well as the aspirations of the era" (xxi). People participated in shaping a domestic ideology that put great value on the home's role in satisfying all the family members' needs.

A quick glance at *I Love Lucy* reveals that the home does not satisfy all of Lucy's needs, nor Ricky's for that matter; the series resonated so fully in the early 1950s because the show acknowledged, albeit comically, the failure of the ideals depicted in popular culture to correspond with people's social experiences. Postwar culture was ripe for such comic treatment because the gap between people's experiences and domestic ideology was more significant in the 1950s than in the earlier decades of the twentieth century. Historian William Chafe summarizes some evidence that leads to this conclusion, "The poll data showed that most citizens preferred to retain traditional definitions of masculine and feminine spheres, even while modifying the content of those spheres in practice" (171). Therefore, when Lucille Ball is quoted as saying, "I'm just a typical housewife at heart" in an article titled "America's Top Saleswomen," she is holding on to a traditional definition of womanhood while experiencing an unconventional career in practice, a celebrity in the public sphere, excelling in the physical comedy that had historically been off-limits to women.

It is not true, however, that Ball was the first pregnant actress to portray a pregnant woman on television. There was a precedent to Ball's pregnancy being incorporated into the television show, contrary to popular perception. Mary Kay and Johnny Stearns starred in the first sitcom, a fifteen-minute show that premiered November 18, 1947, titled *Mary Kay and Johnny*. It was broadcast live, and no kinescopes exist. The same night that Mary Kay missed the live broadcast because she gave birth to a baby boy, December 19, 1948, the television Johnny paced anxiously in the waiting room, and their real-life baby was on the air as their son at the age of ten days. The media coverage of the *I Love Lucy* baby doesn't mention the Stearns precedent, but its audience only measured in the thousands and clearly it did not seep into the cultural consciousness in the same way as Lucy's pregnancy and baby did.[1]

Nevertheless, *I Love Lucy* broke new ground when Ball, Arnaz, and Oppenheimer rejected the sponsor's first suggestion to hide Ball's pregnancy behind chairs and tables and insisted on redrawing the boundaries of what could be represented on television. They transformed what could have ended the series into a new arena for comedy, one in line with the focus on domesticity and family in the wider culture and television's focus on the home and everyday life in particular. Their decision came within a context of changing representations of womanhood, and a move toward making television that was relevant to its audience. Ball was able to maintain her career and still have a family, out in the open; she performed the cultural work of a trickster by being an openly pregnant woman performing on television, which challenged previously held beliefs about the impropriety of pregnancy. It sounds like the setup of a joke, but the network and the sponsor were so concerned about offending the audience that they hired a priest, a rabbi, and a minister to vet the scripts, and they never used the word "pregnant," choosing the French "enceinte" instead. Evoking few complaints and tens of thousands of positive responses, *I Love Lucy* made comedy out of Lucy's cravings, ideas for baby names, mood swings, dreams for the baby's future, Ricky's sympathetic morning sickness and important role as father, and cute maternity clothes (available for sale, along with a line of *I Love Lucy* baby accessories and nursery furniture).

The pregnancy and baby story arc conflated the "real life" of Ball and Arnaz with the Ricardos' fictional life more thoroughly than ever before. In particular, tying together fictionality and reality in the pregnancy shows created an emotional intensity that allowed the audience to be part of a highly mediated but nevertheless moving dramatization of expecting a baby. These reality-based shows let the audience glimpse Ball and Arnaz's private experience as a public representation that reflected

The pillowcase is an example of an *I Love Lucy* commodity in "Ricky Minds the Baby."

and shaped the popular pursuit of marriage and family, and emerged as a metaphor of the baby boom.

The seven pregnancy shows, climaxing of course with "Lucy Goes to the Hospital," followed the conventions already established in the previous season and a half when *I Love Lucy* became a cultural phenomenon. The pregnancy and baby shows brought the series' depiction of the contradictions of middle-class life, marriage, and gender into public discourse. Ball credited identification for the series' success:

> We had a great identification with millions of people. People identified with the Ricardos because we had the same problems they had. Desi and I weren't your ordinary Hollywood couple on TV. We lived in a brownstone apartment somewhere in Manhattan, and paying the rent, getting a new dress, getting a stale fur collar on an old cloth coat, or buying a piece of furniture were all worth a story.
>
> People could identify with those basic things—baby-sitters, traveling, wanting to be entertained, wanting to be loved in a certain way—the two couples on the show were constantly doing things that people all over the country were doing. We just took ordinary situations and exaggerated them. (Qtd. in Andrews 225–26)

The problems Ball mentions all revolve around ordinary, domestic, private life; the solutions to the problems lead back to the essence of the show: the "love" between the husband and wife. Even though the dominant ideal of the postwar era was "companionate marriage," which cast the married couple as a team supporting the husband's career in the public sphere, with the wife firmly ensconced in the private sphere, the actors' collaborative marriage shows through.

Because there was so much media coverage of Ball's pregnancy and rumors that it would be worked into the show, audiences expected that Lucy would tell Ricky she was expecting.

71

In the episode "Lucy Is Enceinte," dramatic irony heightens because the viewer has knowledge that Ricky doesn't; this intensifies when Lucy tries to tell Ricky the news, but obstacles prevent her. The episode climaxes in Ricky's nightclub, with an understandably emotional Ball and Arnaz filming the scene. The setup is one of Davis and Carroll's best: Ricky receives an anonymous note that a woman wants to tell her husband they are expecting a "blessed event" and Ricky moves from table to table to find the couple as he sings "Rock-a-Bye Baby." He reaches Lucy and after an emotional flicker of understanding sings "We're Having a Baby," flubbing the song lyrics as he walks around the stage with a tearful Lucy. The episode concludes with a close-up of the crying and laughing couple. They did another take and filmed the "happier" ending in the script, but it paled next to the first take, and was not used.

This moment is significant because we are watching the actors, not the characters. A more cynical view might be that this "moment" is not authentic but just another layer of artifice and manipulation of the audience, and of course the intimacy established in this scene grows out of a familiarity with the people on-screen that had been skillfully constructed in material that evolved from the intimate moments of everyday life. However, in order for the creative team to choose the take in which the actors were choked up and have it work, there had to have been a long setup to this moment, paved with a hybrid of fictionality and reality that transcends both.

The scene itself plays with the boundaries between the binary oppositions of public and private, and artifice and reality. The camera position as Ricky searches for the parents-to-be from table to table is from the audience, as if the viewer might be next, encouraging our identification as a live audience member (reinforced by the laughter of the studio audience that blurs with the diegetic laughter of the club audience).

The self-reflexive strategy of letting the audience in on both the joke and the seriousness runs through the pregnancy episodes, most interestingly in how Ball's pregnant body was photographed and comedy made out of what it could and couldn't do. There were only scattered moments of Ball's trademark physical comedy in the episodes filmed during her sixth and seventh months of pregnancy (and then the show went on hiatus), but those moments are significant. In "Ricky Has Labor Pains" (January 5, 1953), Lucy can't hoist her body out of a chair to answer the ringing phone. She cleverly pulls the coffee table to her with her feet, upends it, and uses it to get up. In this gag, she is not only a pregnant woman seen in public, continuing to work, but she circumvents her pregnant body's limitations competently and resourcefully. Note that in the first frame, Lucy is reading a magazine with a cover story about *I Love Lucy*!

Ball breaks new ground by making pregnancy funny in "Ricky Has Labor Pains."

The convergence of reality and fictionality suggested by Ball's comic use of her pregnancy came to fruition on January 19, 1953, when both babies were born. In the morning, Lucille Ball had a scheduled cesarean section, and that night, the episode "Lucy Goes to the Hospital" (which had been filmed November 14, 1952) was broadcast. The January 19, 1953, *Newsweek* cover story, "Desilu Formula for Top TV: Brains, Beauty, Now a Baby," describes the synchronicity: "If all goes well, newspaper readers all over the country will be treated on Jan. 20 to the story of Mrs. Arnaz having a baby—the morning after they see Mrs. Ricardo go to the hospital on TV. All this may come under the heading of how duplicated in life and television *can* you get."

Because no one knew the sex of the Ball-Arnaz baby, they couldn't count on the fictional baby being the same sex as the real one, and so it was kept secret that the Ricardo baby would be a boy. The pregnancy episodes play on this uncertainty, and the sex became a topic of popular speculation. Examples of the many headlines reporting the births highlight the elision of fiction and reality: "Lucy Sticks to Script: A Boy It Is!" in the *New York Daily Mirror* (January 20, 1953), "TV Was Right: A Boy for Lucille" in the *Daily News* (January 20, 1953), and "What the Script Ordered" in *Life* (February 2, 1953).

Interestingly, none of the many articles written at the time mention the plot of the episode, just that the baby was born. "Lucy Goes to the Hospital," broadcast to an unprecedented forty-four million Americans for a 71.7 Nielsen rating, mere hours after the real Ball-Arnaz baby had been born, focuses more on Ricky than on Lucy; Ball cut back on her filming schedule as her pregnancy progressed. The episode begins with Ricky studying a book titled *Masks of West Africa,* trying to choose the makeup for his new show that opens that night. He quickly shifts his attention to Lucy when she tells him the baby could come at any minute. Of course, when the moment arrives for Lucy to go to the hospital, Fred, Ricky, and Ethel panic to excellent slapstick comic effect, falling, babbling incoherently, and crashing into each other while a calm Lucy tries to get them to help her out. Here Lucy is the "straight man," the bulk of her seven months pregnant body providing the comic backdrop, as it does in the next scene when a calm Lucy walks into the hospital carrying her own suitcase and nervous Ricky in a wheelchair.

The comic reversal, and incorporation of long-standing jokes about nervous fathers-to-be, is further extended when Ricky doesn't want to leave the hospital for the club until the last possible minute, and so he puts on his "voodoo" makeup at the hospital. Remember, this is 1953, and unlike now when fathers are often present at their children's births, Ricky and Fred are in the fathers' waiting room; Lucy is somewhere behind closed doors under the care of doctors and nurses. All Ricky can do is wait for the nurse to inform him that he is a father. Ricky emerges from a bathroom still wearing his normal clothes of sport jacket and slacks and carrying a briefcase, but wearing the wig and with his face painted for the "voodoo number," a study in contradictions. He scares Fred, then, oblivious, terrifies a nurse who goes off to find the police, and still unaware of the effect of his appearance, he leaves for the club. At the dress rehearsal of a call-and-response drum number, he gets the phone call that he's a father! He rushes back to the hospital in full makeup and costume, seemingly unaware of his appearance. The nurse, a police officer, and an orderly apprehend him as he comes to see his newborn son, but then Ethel identifies him and seeing his son for the first time, Ricky faints!

Ricky is so caught up in being a new father that he has absolutely no self-awareness; even though the father's role in the birth and at the hospital seems curiously disconnected by today's standards, the entire pregnancy arc portrays Ricky as highly engaged, including the sympathetic "labor pains." In the episodes that follow, there are distinct scenes in which Ricky takes care of the baby, like the lovely scene in "Ricky Minds the

Ricky is the center of attention in "Lucy Goes to the Hospital."

Baby" (January 18, 1954) when he tells Little Ricky the story of Little Red Riding Hood in Spanish. The episode concludes with Ricky fainting, again playing up the image of the new father adrift in the world of new responsibilities and roles.

Desi Arnaz, Ricky Ricardo, Ethnicity, and Race

How curious that Ricky is represented as so different in "Lucy Goes to the Hospital," so "Other," not only to Lucy's American-ness but to all things civilized. He is more than an immigrant, he is a bogeyman, and restrained by the gun-toting police officer and orderly before he can explain that he really does belong there. How can we make sense of this very strange representation of Ricky in "Lucy Goes to the Hospital," an image that perhaps speaks to the experience of otherness that provides another important cultural context for the series? From the original inception of the series, when CBS executives said that no one would believe a marriage between an "all-American"—meaning white—woman like Ball and a Cuban, to the importance of Ricky's otherness in his language, reactions, and career, Arnaz's ethnicity provides an undercurrent of tension in the series that is on the one hand essential to his role as a Latin bandleader in the performance realm of the show, and, on the other, mostly used as fodder for comedy or ignored. Nevertheless, it erupts occasionally, paralleling how sexism sometimes comes to the forefront.

Arnaz's status as "Other" because of his ethnicity is one of the undercurrents of Lucy TV. The discourses around ethnicity, and, I would argue, by extension and metaphor, of race, are not as explicitly represented as those of gender, but they are present and persistent, and in certain episodes, like "Lucy Goes to the Hospital," they become prominent. Moreover, Arnaz makes musical and visual connections to the African roots of Cuban music and culture, especially through drumming, masks, and his signature number, "Babalu."

Desi Arnaz and the Latin Music Craze

Like his character Ricky, Desi Arnaz occupied liminal territory "betwixt and between" white and nonwhite in 1950s American culture. Arnaz's star image was based on his Cuban ethnicity and constructed in the context of the Latin lover type. Desiderio Alberto Arnaz y de Acha III, as he was named, was born into one of the richest and politically powerful Cuban families under Gerardo Machado's dictatorship. Arnaz's father had been the mayor of Santiago de Cuba and served in the House of Representatives. Arnaz's father was jailed after the 1933 revolution led by Batista and other military, and their family lost their property and wealth. The family ended up exiled and impoverished in Miami when Arnaz was sixteen. He did odd jobs, including cleaning bird cages, and got a gig singing in a Miami nightclub, where influential bandleader Xavier Cugat saw him and hired him to sing in his band.

Arnaz learned a lot from Cugat, who led the popularization of Cuban music in the 1930s and 1940s. Cugat realized that authentic Cuban forms like the son and rumba had to be made more like familiar foxtrots in order catch on, and his orchestral arrangements shaped a popular taste for Cuban music. He explained, "I played melodic foxes and gradually insinuated the claves and maracas to soften them" (qtd. in Pérez 204). Most importantly, Arnaz learned from Cugat's charismatic stage persona that relied on heavily accented English and a charming embodiment of Latino ethnic identity. When viewing footage of Cugat from the 1930s, it is easy to see where Arnaz and then Ricky Ricardo got his act, but eschewing the guitar and bringing the sexier, vibrant conga drum to the forefront was Arnaz's breakthrough.

It is difficult to overestimate the influence of Latin music in mainstream popular American music in the 1930s, 1940s, and 1950s. As Louis A. Pérez explains in *On Becoming Cuban,* "Between the 1920s and 1950s Cuban music was a pervasive force in the development of popular dancing in the United States. North American appropriation of Cuban musical idioms was accompanied by adaptation and alteration, largely commercial transformations to meet local market conditions. The music arrived loaded with images, and therein lay its appeal: license to deploy energies associated with the tropics. In the course of successive adaptations and arrangements, substance mattered less than form, from which emerged the representation of 'Cuban' on North American terms" (198).

Arnaz soon formed his own band and gained national fame when he started the conga craze, which became a national dance rage and a wildly popular music style in the late 1930s.

Remembering the *comparsas* (processions) of his childhood in Santiago de Cuba, he and his conga drum led the audience in a processional line, doing a fun and easy dance with a kick accenting every fourth beat. Interestingly, Arnaz's father had issued resolutions to suppress the parades called congas in 1925 when he was mayor of Santiago de Cuba during the Machado crackdown on African drums (Sublette 370). This success propelled him out of Miami and first to New York, where he was cast in a Broadway show that culminated in a conga song and dance number, *Too Many Girls,* and then to Hollywood in 1940 for the movie version of the show. Ball and Arnaz met on the set and began their romance immediately.

Too Many Girls was one of the many movies made as part of the Good Neighbor Policy of the 1930s and 1940s intended to foster positive relationships with Central and South American countries and discourage their alignment with the "Axis" powers of Germany, Italy, and Japan. The many Latin-themed musicals that gained popularity in the 1940s and early 1950s, which starred, among others, Arnaz, Cugat, Fernando Lamas, and most famously Carmen Miranda, originated in Hollywood's version of celebrating Latino cultures and portraying happy and harmonious pan-American relationships. *Tropical Trip,* the musical quiz radio show Arnaz hosted in 1951, was similar in spirit, with a grand prize of a vacation to a different Latin American country each week.

The Latin bandleader type developed by Cugat had its roots in the Hollywood ethnic stereotype of the Latin lover, blending exoticism, aristocratic worldliness, and most importantly, sexual knowledge and virility; *I Love Lucy* refers to his movie star persona in the story arc in the third and fourth seasons when Ricky is cast as the lead in the Hollywood film *Don Juan.* Like other versions of ethnic stereotypes in popular culture, "the Cuban bandleader" popularized by Cugat and then Arnaz was essentialized, with the stereotypically ethnic aspects of the character type reinforced and everything else denied. The typecasting as a Latin bandleader would prove both profitable and limiting for Arnaz; he certainly made the most out of it and then retreated behind the camera into the business side of the industry to move beyond the ways he was perceived.

As a member of the ruling elite before the 1933 power shift in Cuba, Arnaz had a privileged childhood, but that changed dramatically when his family ended up poor and in exile in Miami. As an immigrant, as someone whose first language was not English, and specifically as a Cuban, Arnaz faced prejudice and stereotypes based on his nationality and ethnicity throughout his life, even as he parlayed that identity into becoming one of the most famous Cuban American and Latino celebrities for many years.

At a time when there were virtually no African Americans or other people of color on television, and the few who were visible were horribly stereotyped, here was one of the stars of the most popular television show speaking Spanish, speaking English with an accent, and making his Cuban ethnicity central to his character. Perhaps the image of Arnaz in the "witch doctor" makeup illustrates the experience of racism articulated in Arnaz's experience of Cubans being perceived as not white, and the fears of miscegenation that fed into racial segregation.

Among the many ways to read, or interpret, the character of Ricky Ricardo in terms of race and ethnicity, scholars Gustavo Pérez Firmat and Alberto Sandoval-Sánchez arrive at two very different ones. Pérez Firmat celebrates Desi Arnaz in his autobiographically grounded exploration of Cuban American culture, claiming that "Surprising as it may seem, Desi Arnaz's TV character has been the single most visible Hispanic presence in the United States over the past forty years" (1). Pérez Firmat continues, "Ricky Ricardo is the tutelary spirit, the *orisha* of Cuban-American culture. He embodies an openness to otherness, a liking for unlikeness that defines Cuban America as a whole." In addition to the long-lasting character of Ricky, Pérez Firmat counts Desilu among Arnaz's accomplishments and also takes

Arnaz's *A Book* seriously as an immigrant autobiography in the tradition of "a *vivo's* bio, a picaresque tale that recounts its protagonist's rise in the world" (12).

In contrast, Alberto Sandoval-Sánchez is more critical of how Desi Arnaz represents "the 'Latin other' as a *racial* other" (51) and reads the "Lucy Goes to the Hospital" episode as being about racism, calling it "the blackface episode": "a distorted and grotesque masquerade that articulates racist practices within the domain of comedy and performance. Blackface impersonation converts the racial other into an object of humor. What attempts to be amusing and entertaining inscribes a vulgar and demeaning deformation of the racial other, and establishes power relations." Nevertheless, Sandoval-Sánchez concludes, "Ricky/Arnaz was able to bring a black man into a forbidden zone [the hospital and the television screen] by means of blackface, just as he had been able to bring a 'Latin' man into the forbidden zone of an interethnic marriage, one which was perceived as an interracial marriage" (52–53 and 53–54).

This provocative reading makes many valid points, but after studying the episode carefully, I question whether the makeup is actually "blackface." Ricky's face does not appear any darker, and it is not "blacking up" like in minstrelsy. So, how do we read, or interpret, Arnaz's participation in this? One possibility is that as a white-identified person, born and raised in the ruling elite, he may have shared the widespread racial prejudice of the 1950s. Another possibility is that he thought of the costume and makeup as a "tribal Indian chief," as he recalled in his autobiography. Still another is that he willingly participated in portraying Cuba as exotic and primitive, a commodity for American tourism, to further his career and for his own individual benefit. Perhaps he was willing to don the mask of the clown because behind the scenes, he was the boss. Another possibility is that with Ball unable to do the physical comedy because of her pregnancy, the writers came up with a parallel comic costume and makeup getup for Ricky, equally ideologically revealing for ethnicity as Lucy's so often are for gender and class, and Arnaz was glad to showcase his considerable comedic talents. It is impossible to know for sure with such scant evidence. What do you think? How do you "read" Ricky in this episode?

On the other hand, it is certainly possible that Arnaz's experience of prejudice in America, of living through the insult of originally being rejected as a possible costar for his actual wife's television show because the industry insiders didn't believe the "American public" would accept a Cuban married to an "all-American girl" like Ball, compounded with all the ways people treated him as "the Cuban," as if that was his whole identity, did make him aware that he was crossing boundaries that others, without his celebrity and wealth, could not. If we extend Sandoval-Sánchez's reading and view Ricky as a trickster figure in this episode, by incorporating Pérez Firmat's admiration of Arnaz's accomplishments, we can see him performing an impersonation that violates social boundaries to call attention to the categories of race and ethnicity.

Moreover, the musical choices he made on the show, which were his to make, clearly connected Cuban music to its African rhythmic roots. Ricky Ricardo/Desi Arnaz (and in the purely performance numbers, it is hard to distinguish the two) had two performance modes in the club: one was smooth and tuxedoed, the elegant, aristocratic Latin crooner, wrapped in the charms of European "civilization," and the other was the conga drummer, often represented by the African mask. There were very exciting moments in *I Love Lucy* when Ricardo/Arnaz would take a drum solo and almost explode physically out of his tuxedo or suit: loosening his collar, opening his shirt, shaking his head so his hair fell away from its carefully combed-back style. In many of the club scenes, Arnaz physically and performatively embodied the tensions in Cuban music between the African drum and Spanish guitar, much in the same way Ball embodied the tensions of beauty and comedy in female

The "Other" faces of Ricky Ricardo/Desi Arnaz.

performance, or an anxiety of competence around discourses of women's work.

Cultural Appropriation

I have not been able to find any information about how the plot for the episode "Lucy Goes to the Hospital" evolved. It was obviously not based on a radio script from *My Favorite Husband,* as so many *I Love Lucy* episodes were. The autobiographies of the key people are silent on this issue and all focus on the timing of the episode being aired on the very day that Ball and Arnaz would have their baby, and on which sex to make the baby.

In Arnaz's account, he misremembers the getup and focuses instead on gender, on his deep desire for his baby to be a boy: "You probably couldn't see my tears through that crazy makeup and headdress of a tribal Indian chief that I had on, but my eyes were full. I was thinking that in ten or twelve weeks I would be in a real maternity ward waiting to hear our baby had been born and was healthy. Of course, I was really praying our baby would be a boy, but not for the sake of the show. . . . If I didn't have a son, that would be the end of the Arnaz name" (283).

More than anything, this episode represents to me how central cultural appropriation was in Lucy TV, and in American culture in general. There were a plethora of "othered" costumes and disguises on I Love Lucy, including "The Indian Show" (May 5, 1953), in which Ricky's theme for the show at the club is a Native American number. All the stereotypes are reinforced with costumes, makeup, a book Ricky and Lucy read about "Blood Curdling Tales" of attacks and scalpings on the prairie. When Lucy sees an "Indian" show up at her apartment (in costume and makeup), she screams. Later, while everyone else is rehearsing the show, Lucy is stranded in the house with the baby. She strolls the baby to the club even though it is miles, in time to see Ricky rehearsing a romantic song, "By the Waters of Minnetonka" with an "Indian" woman. Jealous, she connives to replace the singer, and appears in the show in the comic finale—with the baby strapped to her back in a papoose child carrier. Her cross-race impersonation gives her a freedom that a white American woman does not have, to have a public role and take care of her baby at the same time. Interestingly, this episode is not shown in syndication in Canada because of its depiction of native people.

This is typical of how American culture is a process of cultural appropriation, which on the one hand shows an interest in a "foreign" culture, but on the other hand obscures the differences between specific Native American peoples in favor of a hodgepodge "Indian," and rips the music out of its original context for its exotic primitive appeal; it is precisely the process that took authentic Cuban music and made it into a foxtrot. Ricky introduces the song as "one of the most beautiful Indian numbers ever written," and it is an interesting example of cultural appropriation. Composer Thurlow Lieurance based the piece on a Sioux love song he heard in 1911 on the Crow Reservation in Montana. What's fascinating here is how Ricky, who represents the non-American other, turns to different themes for his shows at the club, and that this appropriation is shown as essential to mainstream culture. It is as if the Tropicana itself is the site of otherness from which Arnaz and Ricky's appeal originates. Arnaz had used an African mask similar to the one he models his voodoo makeup on in the birth episode in an earlier episode, "Cuban Pals" (April 21, 1952), which highlights Cuban music and its connections to Africa, or what stands in for Africa, the primitive, sexual, and possibly violent as articulated by the mask or the voodoo makeup on which it is based.

The way that Ricky's accented English is portrayed on the show is equally complex. Clearly, it is one of the central sources of comedy in the show; there are jokes based on his pronunciation in every episode. However, the writers quickly realized that the audience laughed only if Lucy, not the other characters, made fun of Ricky's accent. Unlike the benevolent patriarchs of other 1950s television shows, Ricky does not know best in every case, although he is certainly portrayed as successful, talented, and competent in his profession. Arnaz recalls in his autobiography, "It helped when I overemphasized the acceptable Latin use of hands and arms when I was excited. It was also handy to let my eyes pop out of their sockets. Most of all, the rat-tat-tat-tat parade of Spanish words helped me tread that thin line between *funny* mad and *mad* mad" (310).

Pérez Firmat suggests that *I Love Lucy* expresses "heteroculturalism," an interest in and love for otherness. Extending Pérez Firmat's idea, the whole show is really about otherness. Ball and Arnaz play out a fantasy of a "normal" life with a one-career marriage, distinctly different from their true professional lives. The constraints of "typical" American domestic life—budgets, the stresses of working (or not working), ambition, consumer desire, the pursuit of happiness—are all romanticized in *I Love Lucy*. The show makes comedy out of how men and women are different, how native-born and immigrant Americans are different, how regular people and stars are different. Lucy wants what she does not and cannot have; she desperately wants Ricky to be different from what he is, and he often wants her to be different, even if the show also suggests that her zaniness is what attracts him. At the same time (this is comedy, after all, and a trickster story cycle, too), there are the stresses and delights of marriage and domestic life, the centrality of love, and depiction of the good life in America. Nevertheless, it is intriguing to consider *I Love Lucy* as an allegory of celebrating difference, of heteroculturalism, of intermarriage and miscegenation, and in what would emerge as one of the major social movements of the next decade, of desegregation and integration.

Lucille Ball Is "Red"

I Love Lucy also intersected with another side of American life in 1953, albeit not in the fictional world of the show. America's favorite redhead Lucille Ball was the face of television and suddenly "red" took on a whole new meaning with Ball's investigation by the House Un-American Activities Committee for Communist ties during the anticommunist fever of the 1950s. In April 1952, Ball was questioned at a closed meeting of HUAC. She was cleared, and the hearing remained secret.

Although Ball thought the inquiry was over, she was recalled to a closed hearing in September 1953, and this time it did not remain a secret. First, nationally syndicated Hollywood reporter Walter Winchell, long an influential and famous radio and television gossip columnist, ended his Sunday night radio show with a "blind" item that "the top television comedienne has been confronted with her membership in the Communist Party." The next day, Winchell's nationally syndicated newspaper column repeated the same accusation, and newspapers nationwide picked up the story, almost as if the puns of America's most famous redhead being a "red" were too much to resist. Four days later, the day Ball and Arnaz were scheduled to film the first show of the new third season of *I Love Lucy,* the *Los Angeles Herald-Express* newspaper had a huge, four-inch headline printed in red: "LUCILLE BALL NAMED RED," and reproduced Ball's 1936 voter registration affidavit, but with the CANCELED stamp sneakily removed.

At issue were two documents: a voter registration affidavit and a list of Communist Party State Central Committee members that included her name. The affidavit, which clearly has her signature, showed Ball's intention to vote for the Communist Party candidate in the 1936 primary; the affidavit was canceled in 1938 because Ball never voted in the election. Ball explained that she had only filled out the card to humor her grandfather, who was a member of the Communist Party, and who insisted that she, her mother, and brother all register to vote for the Communist Party candidate, but she never voted. She insisted that if her name was on the list of committee members, it had been put there without her knowledge.

On the night that Ball and Arnaz filmed the first episode of the third season of *I Love Lucy,* neither knew how the public would receive Ball in the wake of the Communist accusations. Ball feared she would be booed. CBS, Philip Morris, and some Desilu people were all nervous, too, and Arnaz decided that if Philip Morris pulled its sponsorship, Desilu would take the half hour to explain Ball's innocence to the American people. It didn't come to that, and by the time the studio audience arrived for the filming as planned, Ball and Arnaz knew that Ball had been cleared at a press conference, and that there would be positive headlines coming soon. This is how Desi Arnaz modified his usual warm-up of the studio audience:

Up to now you have only read what people have said about Lucy, but you have not had a chance to read our answer to those accusations. So I will ask you to only do one thing tonight, and that is to reserve your judgment until you read the newspapers tomorrow, where our story will be. . . . And now the girl to whom I've been married for thirteen years and, who, I know, is as American as J. Edgar Hoover, President Eisenhower, of Barney Baruch, my favorite wife, the mother of my children, the vice-president of Desilu Productions—I am the president—my favorite redhead—even *that* is not legitimate. The girl who plays Lucy—Lucille Ball! (303)

The crowd went wild, clapping, cheering, with the actors crying and hugging.

It turned out that the accusation was something Ball and Arnaz were able to weather, but they didn't know that, and they were very anxious that it could end their careers, as it had for so many others in Hollywood. Many people had been blacklisted without any proof at all, just accusation and innuendo; this was particularly easy when the accused were screenwriters and directors whom most people didn't know. As Ball explained in her autobiography, "I was one of the lucky ones. For a long time, people in Hollywood couldn't get a job because of unfounded and vicious smear rumors. If news of my [1936 voter] registration had been revealed during the worst witch-hunting days—between 1945 and 1950—my career probably would have been finished" (233). In fact, the blacklist was alive and well in 1953 and held sway until 1958, when some blacklisted writers were hired for television and given proper screen credit. And it was in 1954 that Senator Joseph McCarthy brought his red scare to the television screen when the new network ABC televised the Army-McCarthy hearings live and, in a precedent that continues to shape television coverage of breaking events to this day, in their entirety.

Many careers had been tainted or lost for far less than this. The Hollywood Ten, the name given to the group of people cited for contempt of Congress because they refused to answer questions at the HUAC hearings in 1947, served six to twelve months in prison. Remember, being a member of the Communist Party was not actually a crime, and although there were some criminal charges and convictions, the power of the witch hunt and the blacklist was economic, professional, political, and creative. All CBS employees had to swear a loyalty oath and be crosschecked against a list of purported left-leaners and Communists in the film and television industries.

For the most part, the witch-hunting was about innuendo, reported testimony by witnesses pressured to name names of Communists, but here was a piece of physical evidence with Ball's name and "Communist" on it. It was not only Ball whose career was threatened but everyone associated with Lucy TV. Earlier in February 1953, CBS and Desilu had signed a record eight million dollar, two-and-a-half-year deal, and that too was in jeopardy, as well as movie deals, endorsements, and the entire Desilu company, which had expanded to produce over six million dollars gross of filmed series in 1953.

Ball's encounter with the anticommunist fervor of the 1950s only lasted a week in the public eye in September 1953. The voter registration card was seventeen years old, and there were no new allegations. Ball was able survive the accusations in part because she and Arnaz had well-placed friends in the media who could help them spin the story their way, but mostly because as scholar Thomas Doherty summarizes in his book about television and the blacklist, "From the episode of the redhead and blacklist, the lesson learned was that while the small fry were hooked and gutted, the big fish would be tossed back" (59). The bottom line was that Ball's career could withstand the controversy because she was such a big star. Ball and Arnaz's journalist friends, like James Bacon, the Associated Press reporter who was the only member of the press allowed to ac-

89

company Arnaz in the fathers' waiting room during the birth, helped out by covering a press conference by committee member Congressman Donald Jackson saying the committee had cleared Ball.

The baby boom, anxieties about race and difference, and anticommunism: all of these cultural trends reflected and shaped postwar ideals about conformity, normality, and containment. From the privileged position of hindsight, we can see that there were cracks in the facade of 1950s American culture that were evident in a cultural text like *I Love Lucy*. Stars like Ball and Arnaz, with considerable economic and cultural capital, were able to widen those cracks and squeeze through, creating precedents for others. Looking closely, we can glimpse the seeds of the issues of feminism, civil rights, and open criticism of the government that erupted in the 1960s and 1970s. Hegemony—the process by which participants in a culture internalize the values and ideals that keep the dominant group in power—is not a stagnant thing, but is constantly evolving and shifting, like the sea. There are different currents within it, as well as the cycle of the tides, with their emerging and residual aspects. A big change far away can affect the entire ocean. By exploring some of the cultural tides and currents that were emerging and receding in 1953, like the baby boom, discourses of ethnicity and race, and the anticommunist hearings, we can better understand how *I Love Lucy* resonated in postwar American culture.

The End of *I Love Lucy* and Beyond

"In" Hollywood

I Love Lucy ran for six seasons in the half-hour format, and then there were thirteen one-hour specials broadcast in 1957–60, which are sometimes referred to as the seventh, eighth, and ninth seasons of *I Love Lucy,* but were actually called *The Lucille Ball-Desi Arnaz Show.* In the first three seasons, *I Love Lucy* focused first on the everyday lives as a couple of Lucy and Ricky, then on the pregnancy, then on life after the baby (which often was just like life before the baby). In the fourth season, there was a big change: Lucy, Ricky, Ethel, and Fred "go" to Hollywood. Of course, the show had always been produced in Hollywood; its setting in New York City was more convention than reality, mirroring the other shows that were broadcast from New York. By setting the show in L.A., the writers had a whole new canvas on which to work: the land of celebrity. They also set up a framework for generating new ideas, by changing part of the situation of the situation comedy, putting the characters in new environments, while keeping the familiar well-loved characters and the dynamics of their relationships.

A fascination with fame and celebrity was a major theme of *I Love Lucy* from the beginning. Even though Ricky is a struggling bandleader in the earlier episodes, he is recognized and known, unlike Lucy, who is anonymous. Lucy's desires to be in the show—to be seen, to be more than just an ordinary person—fuel many plots. For Lucy, everyday life takes on the qualities of performance, with costumes, impersonations, and planned-out scenarios (which rarely go as she intends), but in order for the dynamic of inequality—of otherness—to be maintained, Lucy remains connected to the audience, not the performers. This is Lucy's position, the position of the trickster as outsider, looking in jealously from the outskirts, wanting to be included, whether in the show, in business, or simply in Ricky's attention.

There was criticism during the third season that the successful formula of *I Love Lucy* was growing stale. In *New York Daily News* critic John Crosby's 1953 opinion, "The *Lucy* shows—let's face it—are beginning to sound an awful lot alike. Miss Ball is always trying to bust out of the house; Arnaz is trying to keep her in apron strings. The variations on the theme are infinite but it's the same theme and I'm a mite tired of it" (qtd. in Sanders and Gilbert 85). The ratings averaged around 61 and the shares were in the low 80s for the fall 1953 and winter 1954, in contrast to the peak ratings of 71.8 and 92 share of the "Lucy Goes to the Hospital" episode broadcast on January 19, 1953. The Hollywood arc did increase the ratings, and the series was still number one when the half-hour format stopped after the sixth season in 1957. In the Hollywood episodes, crossing the lines between reality and artifice was used as a source of comedy and audience pleasure, as Lucy became a fanatical fan, hell-bent on glimpsing celebrities, meeting them, and getting souvenirs, often assisted in her complicated schemes by Fred and Ethel. In his work, Ricky interacts with some stars, and sometimes participates in the star hunting. Here Lucy really is our stand-in, even as the audience knows that Ball and Arnaz are friends and colleagues with the guest stars. With the shift in emphasis from Ricky's live performances in clubs in a fictionalized New York to the movie industry shot sometimes on location in real Hollywood, the series becomes even more of an in-joke, even more of an advertisement for television and film culture. The Hollywood shows practically invite the audience to come to L.A. for a vacation, tour the celebrities' homes, glimpse them by the hotel pool, in the famous restaurants, at all the top sights. Somehow, everyday domestic life has been reconfigured to include stars.

In this way, the Hollywood shows offer an interesting depiction of celebrity that sheds light on the relationship between movies and television in the 1950s. On the one hand, the Hollywood story arc maintains the hierarchy that placed film above television in terms of prestige, but on the other, it shows how the movie industry had already become interdependent with the television industry. As Chris Anderson argues, "Hollywood recognized television's ability to reach into the household, the privileged site of consumer culture, and was as eager as any manufacturer to place its products in the American home" (20). The guest stars in the twenty-nine Hollywood shows were able to promote their current movies, such as John Wayne plugging *Blood Alley,* and the producers were able to pay only scale for the performance (Wayne received $280). In the episodes, the sense that the "real" stars are having a good time comes across, and bolstered by the reactions of the live audience responses, the enjoyable artifice of the star interacting with "ordinary" Lucy plays out. Unlike more recent cameos in which stars make fun of themselves (like on media industry satires such as Garry Shandling's *The Larry Sanders Show* or Ricky Gervais's *Extras*), the stars on *I Love Lucy* were idealized, albeit in an accessible, not haughty or snobby way.

Celebrity and stardom are at the center of media culture,

with some salient differences in how film and television stars are constructed, circulated, consumed, and decoded by audiences and fans.[1] What *I Love Lucy* brings is an example of how stardom and celebrity were constructed in everyday life; *Lucy* writer Madelyn Pugh Davis considered the trip West and the California episodes to have a "universal theme that would appeal to viewers" (88). To be fascinated by stars is normal; to participate in the activity of being a tourist in California, to drive across America with your family, all these are portrayed as typical by association with Lucy's "ordinary" character.

"The Homecoming" (November 7, 1955), an episode from the end of the Hollywood arc, is particularly revealing about celebrity, expanding on the oft-used theme of Lucy's jealousy of Ricky. When the characters come back to New York, everyone wants to listen only to Ricky (and not to Lucy). The stories from the episodes that had featured Lucy at the center become Ricky's stories. When an interviewer wants to get the Lucy Ricardo story, she of course dresses up and puts on her best performance of herself, until the interviewer tells her that she has an important mission in life—to make Ricky happy. It is the ideal of the postwar wife exaggerated, as she imagines herself as others see her, the lucky woman married to Ricky Ricardo and rushes around like an overeager servant. He protests, "I want to be treated like a husband!" and teaches her a lesson by impersonating an obnoxious, demanding "star," ordering her around, until finally things return to normal. In this and many other episodes, the lines between perception and reality blur, suggesting that being a star is no different from being an ordinary person, at the same time that of course being a star is different, or what would be the point? It is like the "Just Like Us!" features in the current celebrity gossip magazines that show photographs of stars doing everyday things, but of course no one is interested in seeing pictures of unfamous "us" getting coffee.

On to Europe

After the success of the Hollywood arc, and the new narrative possibilities created by placing the familiar characters in new environments, the creative team decided that Ricky, Lucy, Fred, and Ethel would "go" to Europe, which was quickly becoming a fantasy vacation destination for the upper middle class. Unlike the "truth" of the Hollywood episodes being really filmed in Hollywood, the European ones were shot in the studio.

By changing the location once again, Lucy's outsider status is amplified, especially when she cannot speak the language or understand the customs. In one of the episodes set in Paris, "Paris at Last!" (February 27, 1956), Lucy is the dupe of two con artists, one who offers her a good exchange rate, but for counterfeit francs, and the other a starving street artist who sells her an "original" painting, one that is also bought by Ricky and Fred and Ethel. Both of the cons revolve around ideas of authenticity and fraud; as a foreigner, taken in by her ideas about Paris, art, and her ability to navigate a new country despite not speaking the language, Lucy is an easy mark. As the American innocent abroad, wanting to avoid tourism and have an authentic experience, Lucy has a great scene in a bistro. Unable to understand what the special of the day is, she inadvertently orders escargots—snails. Wide-eyed with wonder and disbelief at what arrives on her plate, Lucy hilariously guesses that the tongs she is given are to pinch her nose so she can stomach eating the snails.

Another favorite scene from the European arc is in "Lucy's Italian Movie" (April 16, 1956), when Lucy again seeks out authenticity, deciding to research winemaking for a part in a movie called *Bitter Grapes* by getting a job at a traditional vineyard stomping grapes with her feet; that scene is similar to the candy-dipping one from the second season in how Lucy is paired with an expert and, with her plucky optimism, thinks that she can perform a skilled task with no experience. In this episode, Lucy outsmarts herself, because the grapes dye her purple and she loses the part to Ethel. This far outside the domestic sphere of her own home, Lucy is more often the dupe than the trickster.

The familiar and proven sources for comedy are evident in the Europe shows: first, Lucy has to convince Ricky to take her on his European tour, then, there are problems with passports and getting to the ship on time. Once on the tour, Lucy wants a Paris original dress, to be included when Ricky meets the Queen of England, causes an avalanche trapping the foursome in the Swiss Alps, learns how to make wine by stomping grapes in Italy, and dreams the characters are in a musical in Scotland. Some of the comic bits are excellent, including Lucy trying to smuggle a cheese back home by pretending it is a baby.

Just as the Hollywood arc reinforced postwar cultural ideas about travel and celebrity, the European arc played into the image of travel abroad and what it means to be an American. Each episode presented a stereotypical image of the country, solidifying and codifying a postwar cultural map of the rest of the world. Conflicts based on gender differences, expectations of marriage, and Lucy's trickery continued, but by changing the environment, Lucy's screwball impulses and logic were given new territory.

Out of the City and Into the Country

Following the success of shifting the location to Hollywood and then to Europe in the previous seasons, what was to be the final season of the half-hour format of *I Love Lucy* moved the characters to Connecticut. Producer Oppenheimer left the show in the spring of 1956, and Arnaz held the only producer credit. There were other shifts in personnel, and the look of the series in the new Connecticut sets was different, less crisp, and sometimes one of the cameras was out of focus. All the actors had, of course, aged. The dynamic between the characters, especially between Lucy and Ricky and Lucy and Ethel, had deepened over the years, adding even greater humor to the Lucy and Ethel high jinks. There were moments of humor, sometimes word-less, stemming from years of the characters' development. For example, when Ricky and Lucy try to close Lucy's overstuffed suitcase by sitting on it together, it won't close, but then Ethel comes in, sits on it alone, and it shuts. Not a word is exchanged in this gag based on years of Fred making fun of Ethel's weight; Lucy simply pats the innocent-looking Ethel on the shoulder, and the scene plays on. Or, in another example, Lucy's quip, "Ricky is mellowing just as I'm running out of tricks," sums up the endgame of the series.

By wanting to move out of New York City to Connecticut, Lucy's desire lined up with an emerging trend in American cul-ture. In the mid-1950s, there was a mass move out of the cities and into the suburbs, which were being built on what had been mostly farmland, so the new 'burbs were still quite rural. Per-haps the most famous postwar suburb was Levittown, twenty miles from New York City; Levittown has become synonymous with homogeneity and conformity, but at the time it was an in-credibly successful solution to the severe housing shortage after the GIs came home from World War II. The first Levittown was built in 1947, with three more rapidly following. As historian David Halberstam notes, Americans' new location in the sub-urbs meant many changes for American life: "the new auto-con-nected suburb was only half as densely populated as the older suburbs, which had been connected to cities by streetcars. It would change the very nature of American society; families of-ten became less connected to their relatives and seldom shared living space with them as they had in the past. The move to the suburbs also temporarily interrupted the progress women had been making before the war in the workplace; for the new sub-urbs separated women physically from the workplace, leaving them, at least for a while, isolated in a world of other mothers, children, and station wagons" (142–43).

The developments also reinforced racial separation and helped make the suburbs white enclaves by refusing to rent to nonwhites. Moreover, the response to the postwar housing shortage reinforced a "two-tier" policy of subsidized housing started in the Depression in the 1930s that constructed cramped multifamily housing for the poor built by public authorities and more spacious, privately developed single-family housing for white, male-headed families.

Instead of attached houses, or apartments in buildings like the Ricardos had lived in, the single-family house was the new standard of the good life, and Lucy wanted it. The Connecticut that Lucy and Ricky move to is not a Levittown-like suburb, but a more idealized, rural small town of Westport, complete with lawns to mow, barbeques to build, new neighbors with whom to socialize and compete, a Yankee Doodle Day to plan, and new money worries for the Ricardos. When Lucy realizes she can't bear to leave the Mertzes behind, they move to the country, too, and unlike the inhabitants of the real suburbs, their extended, intergenerational family stays intact.

One of the funniest moments in the series, and the gag that got the longest laugh, was in the Connecticut show "Lucy Raises Chickens" (March 4, 1957). Concerns about money lead the foursome to decide to raise chickens, but the scheme falters. Ricky and Fred are mad at each other and the women decide to buy eggs and make it look like their unproductive chickens are doing well. Lucy hides a lot of eggs in her blouse so Ricky doesn't find them, and it is this moment that Ricky chooses to practice the tango, with the big finish of when he pulls her against his chest. In his autobiography, Arnaz remembers how Ball played it:

> She first looked at Ricky with a silly smile on that pitiful-looking face, the big blue eyes dancing from Ricky to the audience and back to Ricky, as if claiming innocence. She then looked squirmishly at her bosom and daintily pulled

her blouse away from it, looked back at Ricky with the same silly smile, shook her torso and her waist a little bit, letting the audience know the broken eggs were finding their way down her body.

When she thought the audience laughter might be easing up a bit, she shook her left leg and foot, which told them the eggs had completed their downward tour and were now all over her, bringing up the laughter louder and bigger than before. (317)

Ball blended physical comedy with her reaction and made it look natural and unrehearsed.

There were seven more half-hour episodes made after the tango one, and then thirteen hour-long specials over the next three seasons called *The Lucille Ball-Desi Arnaz Show,* about the same characters. The last show filmed with a live studio audience, "Lucy Wants a Career" (April 13, 1959), is not only the last stylistically but also provides some closure to one of the long-running themes of the series. This time, Lucy does get into show business, even if the act isn't Ricky's, and is successful, but decides that she misses her family too much and that she would rather be a housewife. The story comes full circle from the pilot episode, and although the episodes in which Lucy tries to get into the act were less frequent than people remember, that was the original concept and Lucy's dissatisfaction was at the core of the series, right along with the love among the main characters.

In "Lucy Wants a Career," the structure is the same as in the half-hour shows, and mirrors "Job Switching." In the first scene, Lucy and Ricky argue, but here in 1959, at the tail end of their marriage, much of the humor is gone and the irritation shows in a way that would have been unthinkable in the more broadly comic early episodes. Lucy complains, "Being a housewife is a big bore . . . cook the meals, do the dishes, make the beds, dust the house, cook the meals . . ." When Ethel and Fred enter, the marital squabble elevates to a battle of the sexes, but this time instead of Ethel going along with Lucy into the world of work, Lucy decides to hire Ethel as a housekeeper and babysitter while she goes out to find a job. Lucy successfully employs trickery to scare off all of the other applicants for the position of "Girl Friday" for an early morning television show starring actor Paul Douglas (appearing as himself). Madelyn Pugh Davis summarizes the plot: "She gets stage fright on her first appearance and makes a shambles of the show and is fired. But the audience loves her because she's so natural, and the sponsor tells Paul Douglas he has to hire her back. She likes having a career, but she finds it keeps her from spending time with her son so she quits. I wonder where that idea came from" (146).

Davis's wry comment at the end suggests of course that the plot was based on her experience as a working mother, and the scene in which Little Ricky calls Ethel "Mommy" articulates the real-world difficulties in what would come to be known in the next decades as "having it all," or juggling home and career. There is a realism to this episode absent from the earlier seasons, when Mrs. Trumbull would materialize on cue to take care of Little Ricky. Here are serious consequences of Lucy's ambitions outside the home, but instead of Lucy losing her job because she is incompetent (again), Lucy finds that not being with her family is making her miserable and she decides to quit. The conclusion has it both ways; Lucy has already decided to quit, but then she also has the kind of comic failure that gets her fired.

This episode replays many of the original themes and foundations for comedy, especially in the climactic scene where Lucy introduces the morning show's sponsor's breakfast cereal "Wakey Flakies" after taking sleeping pills the night before. This scene recalls Ball's fantastic "Vitameatavegamin" drunk act; both are performed for the television camera within the diegesis, or fictional world, of the episode. The script, written by Bob Weiskopf and Bob Schiller, with Madelyn Martin and Bob Carroll Jr. credited as script consultants, is careful to make it clear that Lucy has already quit despite being a big hit on television. Ricky finally concedes, "evidently you have a lot of talent," but then Lucy wails, "I don't like having a job. I want to be a housewife again." Here Lucy finally gets what she has wanted for the past eight years, from the moment in the pilot when she explains to her husband, "You need a pretty girl in your act to advertise the sponsor's product." She achieves success in show business, on television, and an escape from the drudgeries of being a housewife, and this time she chooses to go back to being a housewife. Perhaps the most revealing thing we can say about how the series treated female trickery is that it could never portray a context in which it wasn't necessary, even at the end. All it could do—and this was important in 1950s culture—was to work through the contradictions of the changing social relations of the sexes.

In one way, Ricky's acknowledgment of her talent and her choice to be with her family suggests a conclusion to the series, albeit one that rings false with a little thought. The drudgery of endless housework doesn't disappear. Lucy chooses the ideal of domesticity, not the reality of it, even as she skips off with Ricky, both chanting her refrain from the opening scene, "cook the meals, do the dishes, make the beds, dust the house, cook the meals . . ."

Moreover, the reconciliation scene takes place in a train station, where Lucy and Ricky rendezvous when Ricky is coming home from the club and Lucy is going to her early morning show. The creative team working on the show knew that Ball and Arnaz were having terrible fights and that their marriage was in serious crisis. This scene was based on the real-life situation of their dual career-marriage in the 1940s, when they almost divorced because they barely saw each other, and their solution to work together led to *I Love Lucy*. As often happened,

Time is up for Lucy and Ricky, Ball and Arnaz, and the series, in "Lucy Wants a Career."

the fictional world inverted the real-life inspiration, and Lucy and Ricky skip off back into the Ricardo home, as if that impulse alone would fix everything.

There were only four more installments of the *I Love Lucy* format after this episode, and they are pale imitations of the original inspired formula. Without the live audience, the pacing of the shows is off, the actors' performances are wooden, and the filming techniques get in the way. The interpersonal strain shows, too. The Ball and Arnaz marriage was over in all but name and the actors were no longer living together. Ball recalls shooting "The Ricardos Go to Japan" (November 27, 1959), "In one of our last shows I played a geisha girl. My face was covered with white powder. My eyes were red from hours of weeping. Whenever I looked at Desi, I could feel my expression hardening. Cold implacable hate oozed through every pore, for

Desi, and for myself too" (259). Hardly an ideal environment for comedy!

The Last Show

The last show with the *I Love Lucy* characters and situation, now the hour-long *The Westinghouse Desilu Playhouse Presents the Lucille Ball-Desi Arnaz Show,* was filmed on March 2, 1960. On March 3, Ball filed for divorce from Arnaz; starting on March 4, newspaper stories ran with headlines like "Lucy-Desi Drop 'Love' from Title" (*Journal American,* March 5, 1960) and "Desi & Lucy's Next Job: Divorce" (*Daily News,* March 4, 1960). The facade of the happy couple couldn't hold them together, and just as their marriage and family life had been played out in the public eye, their breakup was, too. Rumors about their rocky relationship persisted throughout the second half of the 1950s, but the news of the divorce shocked many. Ball received thousands of letters. She recalled, "They asked me not to get a divorce. They said, 'Why isn't there something you can do?' They didn't know I had been trying to do it for years. I was painfully aware of the feeling the American public had for Lucy and their need for Lucy and Ricky as a happy family. The awareness held up my decision for a long time, until I couldn't allow it to do so anymore" (qtd. in Andrews 197–98). By all the participants' accounts, filming the last show was a somber experience. Unlike the stormy times the collaborators had weathered over the past nine years, full of yelling and accusations, Ball and Arnaz were barely speaking to each other beyond what they needed to communicate to film the show.

Although the last show, "Lucy Meets the Moustache" was not a series finale, the participants all knew this was the end—of an era, a family, a milestone. Guest star Edie Adams remembered, "Everybody was walking around on glass. The show was written so that Lucy and Desi had as few moments together on camera as possible. The Arnazes were both so obviously happy, and the comedy seemed forced because of it. Lucy would just start crying, or would be holding back tears. She was so troubled. Everyone knew we *had* to get the show in the can because we knew it was over and none of us were coming back to that set" (qtd. in Fidelman 139). The final exchange between Lucy and Ricky was yet another example of the kiss-and-makeup, "Now we're even" resolutions that most often closed each episode. As Ball recalled in her autobiography and witnesses confirm, "When the scene arrived and the cameras closed in for that final embrace, we just looked at each other, and then Desi kissed me, and we both cried. It marked the end of so many things" (260). It is fitting that their marriage and their show, which originated in their desire to save their marriage by working together, which transformed television and gave 1950s America a central story cycle that reflected and shaped domesticity, should end together.

Viewers watching the show air on April 1, 1960, already knew that Ball and Arnaz's marriage had ended. Later, Ball said, "Those last five years were sheer, unadulterated hell. . . . We both knew it was over. But we had commitments to fill" (qtd. in Andrews 217). Arnaz explained in his autobiography that their relationship became a "vicious cycle." "The more we fought, the less sex we had, the more seeking others, the more jealousy, the more separations, the more drinking, which led right back to the more fights, less sex and more seeking others, etc., etc., etc. The cycle was soon completed. Add to this the Herculean effort we had to make to maintain the imaginary bliss of Lucy and Ricky, and our lives became a nightmare" (371–72).

The marriage had ended, but the professional intertwinement had not. Desilu was deeply invested in Ball's musical play *Wildcat* and Arnaz was executive producer of Ball's new television series, costarring Vivian Vance, *The Lucy Show*. Ball married her second husband, Gary Morton, in 1961. Morton was also a producer on the show, and Ball and Arnaz decided it was best to sever their joint involvement with Desilu. In 1962, Ball bought him out for three million dollars, and soon became president of a company that had 1,700 employees and was the largest independent rental studio in Hollywood in addition to producing Desilu-owned television series and movies. Ball always claimed she never had aspirations beyond being a hairdresser, but she ended up being a trailblazer for women in the entertainment business.

Other Lucys

Lucille Ball never played Lucy Ricardo again, but she did play other "Lucys": Lucy Carmichael in *The Lucy Show* (1962–68), Lucy Carter in *Here's Lucy* (1968–74), and Lucy Barker in *Life with Lucy* (1986), and for much of the 1960s, Ball reigned as the queen of television comedy, with high-rated shows and unwavering popularity. Are these series also "Lucy TV"? Yes, because the core of the characters is the same, and the conflicts are often the same.

In *The Lucy Show,* easily the best of the three series, Lucy and Viv, both single mothers, fend for themselves, making hilarity especially with their attempts at home repair. Viv was the first divorced woman character on a television sitcom; the creative team decided to make Lucy a widow because they feared the audience would reject the idea of a Lucy who had divorced Ricky. The emphasis in the first two seasons of *The Lucy Show* (written by the *I Love Lucy* writers Madelyn Pugh [credited as Madelyn Martin] and the "three Bobs": Bob Carroll Jr., Bob Weiskopf, and Bob Schiller), is on the friendship between Lucy and Viv, and their comic scenes, whether they are volunteer firefighters or installing a shower, are filled with the many-layered complexities of close female friendship and the brilliant timing at which they had so long excelled. With the addition of Gale Gordon as Mr. Mooney, the banker in *The Lucy Show,* the writers added a conflictual relationship that brought in some of the issues of male authority that propelled many *I Love Lucy*

105

plots, but without the "love" of marriage. Gale Gordon also played Lucy's mean and miserly brother-in-law (her late husband's brother) Harry and her boss in *Here's Lucy*, again a male figure whose authority Lucy attempts to evade.

The post–*I Love Lucy* Lucys become less credible as they become increasingly inept. The *I Love Lucy* writers, Madelyn and the Bobs, left the show in 1964, and the new writers never understood the importance of the careful logical foundations on which *I Love Lucy* producer Oppenheimer insisted. Lucy Ricardo wasn't terrible at everything; she was remarkably clever and crafty—tricky—even if her schemes often backfired. Lucy Carmichael, Carter, and Barker become increasingly incompetent in a time when women's rights were moving to the forefront of national discourses. These Lucys are independent from men, but when it comes to money or professional success, they lack ability. In *Here's Lucy*, the inclusion of Ball's real-life children as Lucy's children recalls the interplay between reality and artifice in *I Love Lucy*, but having teenage children also ups the ante for the character's competence.

Interestingly, motherhood received very different treatment in the post–*I Love Lucy* series. In *I Love Lucy*, motherhood was hardly ever an inconvenience; Lucy's mother or Mrs. Trumbull from downstairs magically appeared to take care of the baby, or rarely Little Ricky was part of a comic complication, like in the "The Indian Show" discussed in the previous chapter when Lucy ends up incorporating him into her "Indian" costume in a papoose child carrier. In that episode, it seemed that motherhood wouldn't slow down tricky Lucy, but in the series as a whole, it was at the expense of any realistic depiction of parenting. In *The Lucy Show, Here's Lucy*, and to a lesser extent, *Life with Lucy*, some of the real-life stresses of motherhood that Lucille Ball wrote about feeling so keenly in her autobiography became, in a sitcom fashion, part of the shows.

Desilu after *I Love Lucy*

By the end of *I Love Lucy*, Desilu matched the productivity and scope of the major motion picture studios. The three-camera system that Desilu had pioneered and perfected had become the industry standard, and the entire mode of production that Desilu invented in order to make *I Love Lucy* cemented the role of the independent producer and the use of film on television. With its success through the 1950s, earning over one million dollars a year from reruns by the mid-1950s while the series was still in its original network run, Desilu demonstrated the profit that a production company could make from syndicated sales of its properties, and set the business model of investing heavily into production costs because it can pay off if the series is sold into syndication, as Desilu sold the rights to *I Love Lucy* in October 1956 to CBS for 4.3 million dollars. This economic model has shaped the television production industry.

Desilu not only excelled at producing *I Love Lucy* but quickly moved into producing other series for the networks, for syndication, and also rented space and equipment for other producers (like *The Danny Thomas Show*). In late 1957, Desilu made a deal for RKO Pictures film studios properties for 6.15 million dollars, and in early 1958, Ball and Arnaz moved Desilu into studios where they had been under contract when they had first met, making them the owners of thirty-three sound stages, more than MGM or Twentieth Century Fox. Among the hit series that Desilu produced in the late 1950s and into the 1960s were *Mission Impossible, Star Trek, The Lucy Show, Mannix, The Ann Southern Show, Westinghouse Desilu Playhouse, The Texan,* and *The Untouchables.*

In 1962, two years after Ball and Arnaz's divorce, Ball bought out Arnaz and took over as head of Desilu. They worked together on *Here's Lucy,* but there was tension with Ball's new husband, Gary Morton, exacerbated by Arnaz's drinking. In

1967, Ball sold the company to Gulf & Western Industries, and formed her own production company, Lucille Ball Productions.

Still Loving Lucy

Of course, Lucy lives on in perpetuity in syndicated episodes of *I Love Lucy,* now lovingly restored to their original length (with those previously cut yet crucial logical setups back at the beginnings of scenes where Oppenheimer, Pugh Davis, and Carroll so painstakingly put them). The actors are frozen in time, preserved in black and white, never to grow old, divorce, or grow stale. Lucy and Ricky love each other, Ethel and Fred are right there, the world is safe, Lucy is at it again, and the comic high jinks never stop.[2] Seen all around the world, translated into many languages, *I Love Lucy* shows no signs of slowing down in popularity.

In addition to entertaining us brilliantly, the reruns offer today's audiences a fitting backstory to the women's movement of the 1960s and 1970s. Scholar George Lipsitz's term "memory as misappropriation" suggests a show can be popular because it represents the past as people wished it had been. *I Love Lucy* recasts the domestic constraints of the 1950s into something that Lucy's individualism, optimism, and irrepressible insistence that Ricky—and everyone else—acknowledge her as a valuable, talented person, can overcome. By wiggling under, vaulting over, and sneaking past the boundary between reality and fictionality, by playing fast and loose with the various windows between the world and the home that television promised and failed to be, Lucy the trickster delighted postwar Americans and participated in a protofeminist cultural current fomenting in American culture. *I Love Lucy* was indeed a TV milestone that shaped the stories we tell, what makes us laugh, and the audiovisual style that still prevails in television situation comedy. It seems we will be loving Lucy for some time to come.

Chapter 1

1. For overviews of the development of television in 1950s America, see also Anderson; Boddy; Halberstam; Lipsitz; May; Meyerowitz; and Spigel's excellent study.
2. See Spigel.
3. For overviews of the development of the situation comedy up to the 1950s, see Boddy; Haralovich; Landay, "*I Love Lucy*"; Marc, *Comic Visions*; and Schatz. For insight into *I Love Lucy,* there are several autobiographies of the participants: Arnaz; Ball; Davis; and Oppenheimer, *Laughs.* Secondary sources focusing on *I Love Lucy* include Andrews; Brady; Fidelman; and Sanders and Gilbert.
4. Direct address is an interesting strategy in the series. In contrast to the contemporaneous *Burns and Allen,* which included George Burns addressing the camera directly as part of its format, Lucy and Ricky rarely look into the camera. In "The Audition," which is based on the pilot, the camera takes the place of the mirror in the Ricardo's bathroom, certainly a moment of unprecedented domestic intimacy for the small screen, but usually it is when the characters perform in front of an audience or the television camera for a show within the show that we have direct address. However, Ricky often interacts with the spectator in the style of the variety show, sometimes with direct address to the camera as he introduces acts as the emcee at the Tropicana.

5. The animated openings of the episodes featured a cartoon Lucy and Ricky, and sometimes a Philip Morris cigarette pack. In the opening for "Lucy Does a TV Commercial," the cigarette pack transforms into a stage that the cartoon Lucy and Ricky approach, and the pack's wrapper changes into a curtain, which pulls back to reveal the live action of Lucy in the Ricardo living room. See Spigel for an analysis of performance and framing in *I Love Lucy,* and Landay, "Millions Love Lucy," for a detailed discussion of commodification in the series.

Chapter 3

1. The life cycle of a television series hinges on the tension between maintaining the familiar, successful premise and keeping the show fresh and interesting. Series often bring in new characters, or shift locale, like *I Love Lucy* did when the characters move to Connecticut, but then loyal viewers feel betrayed. The phrase "jumping the shark" refers to the moment when a television series abandons its original premise and stems from when the *Happy Days* (1974–84) character Fonzie betrayed the audience and jumped over a shark on water skis.

2. For information about *My Favorite Husband,* see Oppenheimer, *Laughs.* See also various websites that have episode lists, plot synopses, downloads of episodes, and recordings for sale, such as Jerry Haendiges Vintage Radio Logs: www.otrsite.com/logs/logm1042.htm and the LucyLibrary.com site maintained by Gregg Oppenheimer (Jess's son) at http://lucylibrary.com/Pages/mfh-guide.1-13.html.

Chapter 4

1. If the reason why there are not more female trickster figures in world mythology is that the stories stem from patriarchal religions that make sexist assumptions about gender, as Lewis Hyde argues, then when we turn away from premodern mythology and to mid-twentieth-century television narrative, there might be a different outcome. It is my argument that female tricksters are a predominantly modern phenomenon, and that they have appeared in the newest form of American popular culture as those forms have grappled with changes in gender.

2. See Landay, *Madcaps.*

3. For a detailed analysis of "Lucy's Schedule," see Landay, *Madcaps* 161–66.

4. There is still a large market for Lucy memorabilia, collectibles, and

consumer items. See, among many others, www.lucystore.com and www.lucy-desi.com.

Chapter 5

1. See "50 years later, Mary Kay and Johnny recall TV's first sitcom," November 14, 1997, www.news-star.com/stories/111497/art_sitcom.html.

Chapter 6

1. There has been considerable scholarship on the cultural phenomenon of celebrity and stars, from Richard Dyer's 1979 study *Stars*, which focuses on the "star image" as a locus of ideology, to more recent studies that emphasize the cultural work performed by celebrities by scholars including Christine Gledhill, P. David Marshall, Chris Rojek, and Diane Negra.
2. The *I Love Lucy* legacy includes the release of home movies, "lost" material, DVD sets, anniversary editions, documentaries, and other ancillary texts. I consulted on and appeared in the PBS American Masters documentary, *Finding Lucy*.

SELECTED BIBLIOGRAPHY

Albert, Katherine. "Everybody Loves Lucy!" *L.A. Examiner* 6 Apr. 1952: 6–7, 18.

Anderson, Christopher. *Hollywood TV: The Studio System in the Fifties.* Austin: U of Texas P, 1994.

Andrews, Bart. *The "I Love Lucy" Book.* New York: Doubleday, 1985.

Arnaz, Desi. *A Book.* New York: Warner, 1976.

Ball, Lucille, with Betty Hannah Hoffman. *Love, Lucy.* New York: Putnam, 1996.

"Beauty into Buffoon." *Life* 18 Feb. 1952: 93–97.

Benjamin, Walter. "The Work of Art in the Age of Mechanical Reproduction." 1936. *Illuminations.* Ed. Hannah Arendt. Trans. Harry Zohn. New York: Schocken, 1969. 217–51.

Boddy, William. *Fifties Television: The Industry and Its Critics.* Urbana: U of Illinois P, 1990.

Brady, Kathleen. *Lucille: The Life of Lucille Ball.* New York: Hyperion, 1994.

Castelluccio, Frank, and Alvin Walker. *The Other Side of Ethel Mertz: The Life Story of Vivian Vance.* New York: Berkley Boulevard, 1998.

Chafe, William H. *The Paradox of Change: American Women in the Twentieth Century.* New York: Oxford UP, 1991.

Charles, Arthur L. "Now We Have Everything." *Modern Screen* Apr. 1953: 32, 84.

Davis, Madelyn Pugh, with Bob Carroll Jr. *Laughing with Lucy: My Life with America's Leading Lady of Comedy.* Cincinnati: Emmis, 2005.

"Desilu Formula for Top TV: Brains, Beauty, Now a Baby." *Newsweek* 19

Jan. 1953: 56–59.

Desjardins, Mary. "Lucy and Desi: Sexuality, Ethnicity, and TV's First Family." *Television, History, and American Culture: Critical Feminist Essays.* Ed. Mary Beth Haralovich and Lauren Rabinovitz. Durham, NC: Duke UP, 1999. 56–74.

Doherty, Thomas. *Cold War, Cool Medium: Television, McCarthyism, and American Culture.* New York: Columbia UP, 2003.

Doty, Alexander. "The Cabinet of Lucy Ricardo: Lucille Ball's Star Image." *Cinema Journal* 29 (1990): 3–22.

Douglas, William. *Television Families: Is Something Wrong in Suburbia?* Mahwah, NJ: Lawrence Erlbaum, 2003.

Fidelman, Geoffrey Mark. *The Lucy Book: A Complete Guide to Her Five Decades on Television.* Los Angeles: Renaissance, 1999.

Freund, Karl. "Filming the 'Lucy' Show." *Art Photography* 4.6 (1953) www.lucyfan.com/freundfilming.html.

Gould, Jack. "Why Millions Love Lucy." *New York Times Magazine* 1 Mar. 1953: 16.

Gray, Herman S. *Cultural Moves: African Americans and the Politics of Representation.* Berkeley: U of California P, 2005.

Halberstam, David. *The Fifties.* New York: Fawcett Columbine, 1993.

Hall, Stuart. "Encoding/Decoding." *Media Studies: A Reader.* Ed. Paul Marris and Sue Thornham. Edinburgh: Edinburgh UP, 1996. 41–49.

———. Introduction. *Representation: Cultural Representations and Signifying Practices.* Ed. Stuart Hall. London: Sage/Open U, 1997. 1–11.

Hanson, Clare. *A Cultural History of Pregnancy, Medicine, and Culture, 1750–2000.* Basingstoke, UK: Palgrave, 2004.

Haralovich, Mary Beth. "Sitcoms and Suburbs: Positioning the 1950s Homemaker." *Quarterly Review of Film and Television* 11.1 (1989): 61–83.

Landay, Lori. "*I Love Lucy:* Television and Gender in Postwar Domestic Ideology." *The Sitcom Reader: America Viewed and Skewed.* Ed. Mary M. Dalton and Laura Linder. Albany: State U of New York P, 2005. 87–97.

———. *Madcaps, Screwballs, and Con Women: The Female Trickster in American Culture.* Philadelphia: U of Pennsylvania P, 1998.

———. "Millions Love Lucy: Commodification and the Lucy Phenomenon." *National Women's Studies Association Journal* 11.2 (1999): 25–47.

Lipsitz, George. *Time Passages: Collective Memory and American Popular*

Culture. Minneapolis: U of Minnesota P, 1990.

"Lucille Ball: Love Is Her Favorite Career." *Quick* 27 Nov. 1950: 51–53.

Marc, David. *Comic Visions: Television Comedy and American Culture*. Boston: Unwin Hyman, 1989.

———. "Origins of the Genre: In Search of the Radio Sitcom." *The Sitcom Reader: America Viewed and Skewed*. Ed. Mary M. Dalton and Laura Linder. Albany: State U of New York P, 2005. 15–24.

Marc, David, and Robert J. Thompson. *Television in the Antenna Age: A Concise History*. Malden, MA: Blackwell, 2005.

Marshall, P. David. *Celebrity and Power: Fame in Contemporary Culture*. Minneapolis: U of Minnesota P, 1997.

Mast, Gerald. *Comic Mind: Comedy and the Movies*. Indianapolis: Bobbs-Merrill, 1973.

May, Elaine Tyler. *Homeward Bound: American Families in the Cold War Era*. New York: Basic, 1988.

Mellencamp, Patricia. "Situation Comedy, Feminism, and Freud: Discourses of Gracie and Lucy." *Studies in Entertainment: Critical Approaches to Mass Culture*. Ed. Tania Modleski. Bloomington: Indiana UP, 1986. 80–95.

Meyerowitz, Joanne. "Beyond the Feminine Mystique: A Reassessment of Postwar Mass Culture, 1946–1958." *Journal of American History* 79.4 (1993): 1455–82.

Miller, Douglas T., and Marion Nowak. *The Fifties: The Way We Really Were*. Garden City, NY: Doubleday, 1977.

Morehead, Albert. "'Lucy' Ball." *Cosmopolitan* Jan. 1953: 15–19.

Oppenheimer, Jess, with Gregg Oppenheimer. *Laughs, Luck . . . and Lucy: How I Came to Create the Most Popular Sitcom of All Time*. Syracuse: Syracuse UP, 1996.

———. "Lucy's Two Babies." *Look* 21 Apr. 1953: 20–24.

Pelton, Robert D. *The Trickster in West Africa: A Study of Mythic Irony and Sacred Delight*. Berkeley: U of California P, 1980.

Pérez, Louis A., Jr. *On Becoming Cuban: Identity, Nationality, and Culture*. New York: Harper Perennial, 2001.

Pérez Firmat, Gustavo. *Life on the Hyphen: The Cuban-American Way*. Austin: U of Texas P, 1994.

Press, Andrea L. *Women Watching Television: Gender, Class, and Generation in the American Experience*. Philadelphia: U of Pennsylvania P, 1991.

Sanders, Coyne Steven, and Tom Gilbert. *Desilu: The Story of Lucille Ball and Desi Arnaz*. New York: William Morrow, 1993.

Sandoval-Sánchez, Alberto. *José, Can You See? Latinos On and Off Broadway.* Madison: U of Wisconsin P, 1999.

"Sassafrassa, the Queen." *Time* 26 May 1952: 62–68.

Schatz, Thomas. "Desilu, *I Love Lucy,* and the Rise of Network TV." *Making Television: Authorship and the Production Process.* Ed. Robert J. Thompson and Gary Burns. New York: Praeger, 1990. 117–36.

Silvian, Leonore. "Laughing Lucille." *Look* 3 June 1952: 7–8.

Spigel, Lynn. *Make Room for TV: Television and the Family Ideal in Postwar America.* Chicago: U of Chicago P, 1992.

Sublette, Ned. *Cuba and Its Music: From the First Drums to the Mambo.* Chicago: Chicago Review Press, 2004.

"Unaverage Situation." *Time* 18 Feb. 1952.

Wolters, Larry. "They All Love Lucy!" *Chicago Sunday Tribune* 23 Mar. 1952: 6, 25.

Page numbers in italics refer to images.

Printed in the USA
CPSIA information can be obtained
at www.ICGtesting.com
CBHW071925220524
8738CB00028B/334

9 780814 332610